COURTNEY TATE

Unseen Yet Essential

A Resource for Black Women Instructional Coaches

First published by Literary Wonder Publishing 2025

First edition

ISBN (paperback): 978-1-958563-12-0
ISBN (hardcover): 978-1-958563-13-7

Contents

INTRODUCTION

"The moment you feel most questioned is often the moment you've already been called."

— C. Tate

Before the first coaching session, presentations, strategies, and feedback models … there was resistance.

I had just quietly launched Aligned. A simple website with a few of my children's books and my professional development offerings related to instruction. I didn't even have a full client list, just a calling and a sense that God was shifting something in me.

Then the call came.

A billion-dollar company had HR on the line. They'd seen my site and searched my name. And suddenly, they asked questions about what I offered, how I planned to work and consult, how I would get my clients without poaching, and whether I was choosing them or AlignEd. I stood firm, but I was *shaken*. That moment, uninvited and unexpected, could've derailed me. I could've shut everything down. I could've convinced myself that the timing was wrong, that the dream was premature, that I needed to wait until I was "ready."

But what I've come to know is this: Sometimes the resistance is your receipt. Proof that the work in you has already started moving even before you recognize it. This book wasn't born out of theory. It was born out of moments like that. Moments that tested me, stretched me, and ultimately reminded me of the power of alignment.

So, before you dive into the heart of this text, I want you to know:

You don't need to be fully *ready* to be called.

You don't need the title to walk in your authority.

You don't need permission to shift the culture.

You are already positioned, marked, and enough.

Now let's walk this journey together.

Courtney Tate, PhD, The Aligned Coach

The Reality of Black Women in Instructional Coaching

Despite making up a significant portion of the educational workforce, Black women remain underrepresented in instructional coaching and leadership roles (N. N. Johnson & Fournillier, 2021). While we may be offered a seat at some tables, we don't always have a voice in the room. Instructional coaching has become a widely adopted form of professional development designed to improve teacher practice and student achievement. Yet, Black women continue to be overlooked in these roles, facing systemic barriers that limit their access to leadership opportunities.

The underrepresentation of Black women in instructional leadership is not accidental. It is the result of historical and systemic inequities that trace back to the aftermath of Brown v. Board of Education (1954) (Brown, 2005; Foster, 2005; N. N. Johnson, 2024; N. N. Johnson & Fournillier, 2021). Following the landmark decision, Black educators and school leaders found themselves displaced and significantly underrepresented in both classrooms and leadership positions. The desegregation of schools led to the systematic dismissal of highly credentialed Black teachers and administrators, while white educators were chosen to fill those vacancies. This shift severely weakened the pipeline of Black educators entering leadership roles, a reality that persists today.

Although many celebrate the progress of desegregation, the consequences continue to have a stark impact on the educational landscape for Black students, educators, and leaders. Black instructional leaders, particularly women, are often placed in under-resourced schools with lower proficiency rates, expected to lead without the necessary support or infrastructure (Brown, 2005). Meanwhile, leadership preparation programs fail to address the unique challenges Black women face, leaving them without the tools and networks their white counterparts readily access. As a result, Black women in instructional leadership remain marginalized, often excluded from decision- making processes that shape the very policies and practices they are expected to implement.

The Role of Instructional Coaches or the Rise of Instructional Coaching

Today, in the classroom, I see an instructional coach supporting teachers and helping them refine their craft, which is common practice. Following calls for school reform, instructional coaching became one of the most widely used forms of professional development to support teacher development and close achievement gaps (Woulfin, 2018). For the past few decades, educational leaders have searched for ways to close learning gaps, and instructional coaching has surfaced as a powerful means of improving teacher practice. As policies have shifted from No Child Left Behind (NCLB) to Race to the Top (RTTT) and eventually the Every Student Succeeds Act (ESSA), so has the approach to professional development.

With an emphasis on school reform, it became clear that it was time to move from sit-and-get learning sessions to learning that encompasses a more action-based, collaborative, and ongoing approach. This change emerged from the 2015 ESSA, requiring schools to transition from compliance-based training and one-time workshops to a more personalized, evidence-based approach (Darling-Hammond, 2016; Johnson, 2016). Schools have moved into creating ongoing, job-embedded learning, which is well captured through coaching.

Instructional coaching embodies adult learning theory, where adults learn best when their experiences are valued, the learning is relevant, and their voices are acknowledged. These are fulfilled through instructional coaching, which is about asking questions, not telling. Many of you may be able to relate to the feeling of being unprepared for the role or struggling to balance the demands of the role and outside more administrative tasks while focusing on instructional support (Shvieley, 2022).

As schools and leaders refine their coaching models, they must consider what coaching looks, feels, and sounds like in their respective buildings or districts. Instructional coaching is critical to school improvement, providing teachers with individualized support, research-based strategies, and training to enhance their instructional practice. However, the experiences of BWICs remain largely absent from research and discourse, limiting both their professional development and career advancement opportunities. By understanding the challenges and successes of those coaching in their district and the need for coaching, districts can build a more effective coaching program that meets the needs of all educators.

While instructional coaching has no singular definition, it is widely recognized as an in-service professional development model designed to help teachers improve their practice. Studies consistently show the positive impact instructional coaching can have on teacher effectiveness and student outcomes.

Serving in an instructional coaching role, I am sure you have encountered many reactions that show resistance to change or your leadership, such as:

- "I don't need a coach. I know what I am doing."
- "Go ahead. Just tell me what you need me to do."
- "Great, I guess you are here to fix my teaching."

When coaching is not fully understood, some comments can come from misinterpretations and perpetuate a misunderstanding of instructional coaching. Without the role of a coach being clearly defined, teachers may continue to feel as though their role is evaluative, administrators may give them tasks that keep them from actively coaching teachers, and this may lead you to question your own impact.

While you are knee-deep in the work and can feel the frustration of the day-to-day difficulties and mindsets you may encounter, the research reminds us that instructional coaching is meaningful. Through collaboration, reflection, and tailored support, coaching is designed to help teachers improve their craft alongside teachers (Knight, 2011). So, where does this leave Black women serving in instructional coaching roles? Black women in these roles often balance systemic challenges that make success more difficult to attain and are not often explored within the literature. Designed to help BWICs navigate their unique challenges, this book illuminates their experiences while providing strategies for them to lead with confidence. As we examine how the role of a coach fits into the context of educational leadership and schools, we will also investigate what it means to coach while Black.

BWICs face many of the same challenges as their peers, such as defining their roles, balancing administrative tasks, and navigating school dynamics. However, they must also contend with additional burdens, such as proving their competence in ways their white counterparts do not have to, overcoming racial and gender bias, and resisting the harmful stereotypes that frame them as unqualified or aggressive. The lack of targeted training and mentorship for Black women in these roles further compounds these challenges, leaving them to navigate their positions with limited resources and support.

As an instructional coach, I experienced these barriers firsthand. I recall walking into school buildings only to be completely ignored. When I stepped to the front of the room, I was met with skepticism, forced to validate my expertise before being allowed to lead. In contrast, my white colleagues were welcomed without question and granted authority and respect simply by their presence. In conversations with other BWICs, I quickly saw a pattern: our experiences mirrored each other in unsettling ways. We were often met with doubt, held to higher standards, and expected to prove ourselves in ways our white peers were not.

As one coach, Sunflower, shared, *"Trust takes time here. They need to see me in action before they believe in me. Meanwhile, white colleagues are trusted from day one. I have to earn what others are simply given."*

This stark reality made me ask: *Why is this our truth? How do we overcome these barriers? How do we push back against these systemic challenges?*

This book is an attempt to answer those questions. It is a call to action to recognize, support, and elevate the voices of Black

6

women in instructional coaching. Through personal narratives, research, and practical strategies, I aim to shed light on our experiences, highlight our barriers, and provide solutions to help BWICs lead confidently and flourish in their roles. Instructional coaching is a powerful tool for educational equity that must be intentionally designed to include and uplift Black women in leadership.

It's time to rewrite the narrative.

I

Part One:
Understanding the Challenges

CHAPTER 1

The Gaps in Coaching Frameworks for Black Women Instructional Coaches

I expected some resistance when I began leading professional development and instructional coaching across state lines. But I didn't expect microaggressions to become so routine.

I'd walk onto a campus and be greeted with a warm smile, followed by: "Are you the substitute for the day?" When I clarified that I was leading the PD, I'd sometimes get a confused look, like I had disrupted a storyline they'd already written. Other times, I'd still be welcomed, but then came the questions:

"So ... what did you do before this?" "How old are you?"

"Tell me about your background."

And when I chose to answer, the response was usually, "Oh! You're well qualified to lead this work." I often hated that moment. Not because I wasn't proud of my background, but because I shouldn't have to recount my résumé just to be taken seriously. Not when the work always spoke for itself.

What frustrated me most was the energy I had to spend tearing down barriers that shouldn't have been there in the first place. Meanwhile, some of the same people who were questioning me were still struggling to grasp the content they were responsible for teaching. And still, the sessions shifted. The wall would come down. The room would engage. We built something real. But that extra labor I carried into each space? That stayed with me.

That tension or need to prove, re-explain, and justify led me to listen more closely to the stories of other BWICs. I wanted to know if they felt it too. I focused on those working in K–12 buildings because they are closest to the challenges and the change.

This book is for us. To honor our stories, to offer solutions, and to create space.

Because while we may not always change the mindset in the room, we can change how we show up, lead, and sustain ourselves in this work.

In conversations with others, it became clear that my experiences weren't isolated. Many other Black women in leadership had faced the same challenges: being silenced, underestimated, or silently required to prove their worth. No matter how strong their credentials or backgrounds were. These weren't isolated moments. They were patterns that shaped how we lead, how we're perceived, and how long we remain in these roles.

I knew I wasn't alone, but I also knew no one was naming it. The absence of our voices and representation fueled my desire to ask: *Why are the experiences of BWICs so different? And what needs to shift?* Throughout my research, I identified several key challenges that BWICs face that most existing coaching models fail to fully address.

Many scholars and practitioners have developed powerful frameworks that have shaped education, enhanced teacher practice, and improved student outcomes. Instructional coaching frameworks have shaped the field and elevated the importance of coaching as a lever for school improvement. Yet these models were not developed with the nuanced, racialized experiences of Black women instructional coaches in mind. As I conducted my study, a critical gap emerged beyond simply capturing and sharing the stories of BWICs. It became increasingly clear that white men and women have developed the most established coaching models. While these models offer valuable tools, they often fail to account for the unique, racialized, and gendered experiences of Black women in coaching roles.

Why Do BWICs Experience Coaching Differently?

Being a Black woman in an instructional coaching role means navigating the intersection of race and gender, a space shaped by both racial and gendered marginalization.

You are not *just* an instructional coach.

You are navigating biases and barriers that many of your peers do not have to face. You are proving your expertise repeatedly, even when you are the most qualified person in the room. You are advocating for equity, often in environments that resist change. If you're reading this book as a Black woman instructional coach, I imagine you're nodding in agreement. Maybe you're even thinking, why didn't I realize this before?

I had the same realization early in my PhD journey. I felt this in my work, but I hadn't had the words for it yet. Was it just me? Was this something only I was experiencing?

Then, as I conducted my research and listened to my participants' stories, I knew this was not just an individual experience. It was a pattern, a systemic issue. BWICs shape instruction and navigate structures that were not built with them in mind. And most importantly, we deserve better strategies for survival, influence, leadership, and long-term success. That's what this book is about.

This book is intended to uplift the voices of BWICs, acknowledging how their stories are often left out of research and leadership conversations. Instructional coaching is a form of instructional leadership. Yet Black women continue to face barriers that directly impact their work.

While there is existing literature related to coaching, pedagogy, and teacher development, it rarely speaks to the unique racial and gender-based experiences of BWICs. Most coaching content assumes a shared reality for all coaches. But coaching while Black is different.

This book is written for BWICs navigating the complexity of coaching in systems that don't always see them but desperately need their leadership.

It is written for:

- Aspiring BWICs – to offer guidance and insight as you prepare for the role.
- Current BWICs – to validate your experiences and give you tools to navigate them.
- Leaders and Allies – to illuminate the systemic challenges BWICs face and inspire necessary change.

Have you ever felt the need to prove your worth or validate your contributions in your coaching role? Like you've had to speak up repeatedly, only to be ignored or overlooked? If so, you're not alone.

Though Black women make up a small percentage of instructional leaders, those who do hold these roles often share similar experiences and struggles. This book is here to say your leadership matters. Your voice matters. And it's time the field made space for all that you bring.

Five major themes surfaced throughout my study, capturing the unique challenges, strategies, and triumphs of BWICs. These themes reveal the complexity of their experiences but underscore their resilience, leadership, and impact in educational spaces. These included:

1. Redefining their coaching identity
2. Building resilience in the face of resistance
3. Proving their expertise repeatedly
4. Advocating for equity and representation
5. The need for a deep sense of belonging through community.

Each theme reveals a unique challenge and a powerful strategy for thriving as a BWIC.

Redefining Your Coaching Identity

BWICs are constantly reshaping their identity within coaching spaces. Traditional coaching models and success metrics often fail to capture their true impact, forcing them to redefine what success looks like in their roles. Many BWICs shared that they had to push back against imposed narratives, particularly the stereotypes of being "aggressive" or "angry" when they asserted their leadership. Instead of being seen as instructional leaders, they were often positioned as helpers or support staff rather than experts. To navigate this, they had to reclaim their authority and shift perceptions. Success for BWICs isn't just about improving instructional practices; it's also about advocating for systemic change, strengthening teacher mindsets, and fostering culturally responsive learning environments.

"I teach teachers how to fish. I don't just tell them what to do; I show them how to succeed on their own." — Dannie

With a stance of developing a skill set, Dannie faced resistance from those uncomfortable with her leadership methodology. She remained firm in her approach and refused to fit into the leadership box they attempted to confine her to, establishing her voice and identity as an instructional leader.

Why this matters:

When BWICs are seen as fixers or redefining their leadership role to overcome labels and stereotypes placed upon them, it can wear down their confidence and undermine the true purpose of their work. Schools and districts must clarify their vision for coaching and uplifting BWICs as they lead from their expertise. We must trust them to do the job without compromising their leadership style. As you reflect on coaching in your building, *consider who defines the identity of coaches and who is missing from that definition.*

Resilience in the Face of Resistance

Resilience is at the core of what allows BWICs to persist despite resistance from teachers, administrators, and school systems. Many shared stories of adapting their coaching practices when faced with teacher pushback or bias. Some used data to build credibility, while others relied on strong relationships to break down resistance. Phalan, one of the participants in my study, spoke about the importance of recognizing her biases before expecting others to do the same. She acknowledged that, just like her teachers, she carried experiences that shaped her perceptions. By being intentional about relationship building, she was able to approach coaching conversations with cultural awareness and impact. BWICs must often be flexible and strategic, using coping mechanisms such as advocacy, alliances, and self-preservation to sustain their work without losing confidence or burning out.

"I often feel silenced and overlooked by my peers ... I have to work two, three, four, five times as hard to prove I belong." — Sunflower

14

Despite her formal coaching training and administrative degree, Sunflower found her contributions frequently dismissed, especially in predominantly white spaces.

Why this matters:

Silencing often occurs subtly and can dilute the leadership of BWICs if they are not resilient. If BWICs cower to the resistance, the teachers lose access to valuable feedback and ideas that could positively impact their instruction. To counter this, leaders have to intentionally cultivate a culture of coaching, which includes validating the voices of BWICs. As you reflect on coaching in your building, consider whose voice is heard and implemented and whose voice gets ignored in meetings and discussions. Are there systems in place to ensure coaches' words are implemented?

Intellectual Contributions and Proving Expertise

BWICs consistently find themselves in positions where they must prove their expertise despite years of experience and strong instructional knowledge. Many reported being questioned about their qualifications or having their ideas dismissed, only to see those same ideas embraced when presented by a white colleague. The need to overexplain, over-prepare, and repeatedly justify their expertise is a shared reality. However, instead of backing down, these coaches have learned to position their expertise strategically using data, storytelling, and self-advocacy to ensure their voices are heard. They have mastered reinforcing their credibility, ensuring that their knowledge isn't overlooked but instead leveraged for meaningful instructional change.

"I hated to share my rich background ... Aside from the amazing PD, they were about to experience with me, I didn't owe them that." — C. Tate

The experience of having to run through your résumé or being scrutinized and questioned underscores the unspoken expectations to overly establish your value as a Black woman instructional coach.

Why this matters:

Consistently being asked to prove your work or showcase your credentials can convey that you are unqualified or don't belong in the space. Consistently encountering this pressure can result in second-guessing and burnout, especially for Black women. Respect needs to be the norm for all, instead of something BWICs are made to feel they need to earn. As you reflect on coaching in your setting, consider what unspoken expectations or tests Black women coaches are being asked to pass.

Being a Change Agent and Advocate

Many BWICs are the only Black leaders in their schools, carrying both an explicit and unspoken responsibility to advocate for equity. Representation matters, not just for the students they serve but also for teachers who need guidance in recognizing and challenging their biases. Several BWICs in my study shared that their schools exhibited patterns of inequity, whether in student placement, discipline, or access to rigorous coursework. Ivy, for example, noticed a troubling trend: Honors and advanced placement courses had become less diverse, even in a racially mixed school. At the same time, Black and American Indian[EM1] students were disproportionately receiving disciplinary referrals. She took action, using her role as a coach to question these disparities and push for systemic reflection. While change didn't happen overnight, her advocacy sparked conversations that forced administrators and teachers to examine the biases influencing their decisions. BWICs are not just instructional leaders but equity warriors, leveraging coaching to shift mindsets and transform schools.

"I was the only Black leader in the building, which meant students gravitated to me for connection … I wanted to be someone they saw as a point of contact."— Michelle

Michelle realized how important her presence was in her setting. She represented hope and visibility for her students and carried that emotional labor each day.

Why this matters:

Carrying the emotional labor inherent in this role can be deeply depleting, especially when Black women coaches are the only ones left to be everything. Being seen as the fixer on top of their job can impact clarity and longevity in the role. As you reflect on coaching in your setting, consider how BWICs can exist without being superheroes.

Cultivating a Sense of Belonging

Sustaining the work of instructional coaching is impossible in isolation. For BWICs, finding a community of support is not just beneficial—it's necessary for survival in the profession. Many participants in my study shared that their districts did not provide spaces for Black women in leadership to connect, so they curated their own. They built networks across past school districts, leaned on relationships with former colleagues, and sought mentorship from other Black women educators who understood their experiences. Phalan described this as a critical piece of sustainability, having a network where she could process coaching challenges without fear of judgment. These spaces became safe havens where BWICs could share their struggles and strategize ways to navigate the barriers they encountered in their schools.

These themes and this book were inspired by my experiences and those of seven participants from my research study. Each theme emerged from their stories that present a counterstory to the dominant narratives, which mostly don't account for our experiences, and inspired their development.

Why this matters:

When BWICs feel connected, they have more confidence and can feel a stronger sense of purpose in their work. Without community, isolation and self-doubt can kick in, impacting how they show up when doing the work. As you reflect on coaching in your setting, consider whether coaches have a place where they feel seen and heard. Has anything been done to affirm a coach's sense of belonging in this environment?

CHAPTER 2

HERStories: Lived Experiences of Black Women in Instructional Coaching

The stories that follow are not just narratives. They are evidence. Each woman in this chapter opened up her lived experience, allowing me to capture what it truly means to coach while Black. Their stories are filled with challenges, resistance, resilience, and transformation. These HERStories are not filtered. They are layered, emotional, and powerful because they are real.

These HERStories remind us that we are not alone. Our lived realities are not just valid. They are essential.

Sunflower's Journey: Navigating Resistance and Proving Worth

Sunflower has worked in education for over ten years, with the last four and a half years as an instructional coach in two rural school districts. Sunflower was influenced by her grandmother, who worked as an educator and was a caretaker for her while she was growing up. As a child, she often assumed the role of a teacher who created lessons for her younger cousins and helped her grandmother care for them. Although her initial intention was not to be an educator, during her senior year, circumstances in her family changed, and she applied for and received a teaching fellows scholarship. She knew she could at least teach for four years to fulfill her obligations and shift her career later if needed. However, her love for education naturally grew, and she remained in the field.

Sunflower was inspired by her instructional coach's impact on teacher practice from firsthand experience and wanted to broaden her leadership skills without becoming a school principal. After having experiences with her principal, who did not want to give her opportunities beyond the classroom, she accepted a role in another school district as an instructional coach. Sunflower has served as an instructional coach in two school districts for the past four years, gaining new experiences as a Black woman in this role. In her first district, she received little resistance despite being her school's only Black instructional leader.

Conversely, Sunflower serves as a district-level instructional coach in her current district and has experienced more challenges due to a lack of cultural awareness in some of the schools she supports. On her team, she often feels silenced and overlooked by her peers, and it often seems she has to work "two, three, four, five times as hard" as her colleagues to prove her worth to the team. Despite being the only one on the team with formal coaching training and one of two team members with an administrative degree, her contributions are often dismissed, leaving her frustrated. Consistently facing the double standard and needing to prove herself and her knowledge while her white colleagues are not held to the same standard can be discouraging.

When asked how she feels her identity as a Black woman has impacted her ability to advance within her career, Sunflower discussed the positive influence her minority mentors have had. Throughout her career, she has been assigned to Black teachers, leaders, and schools believed to be "difficult," while her white peers are not assigned to those same schools. Currently, being viewed as an "outsider" contributes to the difficulty she faces, adding a layer of scrutiny to gain trust when those who are "homegrown" rarely encounter the same challenges. To remain adaptive, Sunflower has adopted a gentler approach when coaching to establish trust in predominantly white settings where she feels she must "tread lightly." While she is more accepted by teachers in more diverse populations, she finds it easier to build rapport and establish credibility due to their shared experiences, making space for more transparent conversations. In addition, she maintains detailed documentation of her work in case her contributions are called into question, something that her peers do not have to account for.

Sunflower talked about the nuances of navigating her role as a Black woman in an instructional coaching role, highlighting that it was harder to build trust and rapport in predominantly white settings and that there was little support in the district to navigate or acknowledge the challenges she faced. The lack of cultural awareness and low representation of Black leaders drives a lack of inclusivity, which has contributed to her negative experiences as an instructional coach.

Despite her opposition and sometimes oppressive experiences, Sunflower is grateful to have a strong network from which she can draw strength. Her mentor within the district usually encourages her to "let it go" and remain polished and professional. In contrast, her younger mentor outside the district encourages her to speak up against the inequities. The duality of her mentors' approaches helps Sunflower strike a balance to advocate for herself professionally while navigating the complexities of her role. She also has cohort members in her doctoral program and other leaders in surrounding districts to provide perspective and insight.

With her resilience and determination to positively impact teaching and learning, she models a commitment to being a change agent despite the opposition she may face. Despite her experiences, she continues to advocate for more inclusive environments and support for diverse leaders with the desire to pave the way for more minority leaders in the future.

AA's Journey: Breaking Barriers in a White-Dominated District

AA, an assistant principal with over ten years in education and four years working as an instructional coach, reflects on her journey and the impacts gender and race have had on her work. AA maintains a commitment to her work, knowing how impactful her representation as a Black woman in Magnolia has been despite her obstacles. Her inspiration to become an educator was her grandmother and family, who have a strong background in education. Initially, she went to school intending to take a different major but soon switched to education and realized her passion for her work in the field. AA is a pioneer as the first Black math instructional coach in this school district and is only one of two Black instructional coaches. She found her identity played a major role in her experiences as an IC. She often navigated the pressure and isolation from a lack of Black instructional leaders in the district. She feels an unstated expectation to work "ten times harder" to be seen as a credible coach due to her age, experience, and identity as a Black woman. She described instances in which she encountered resistance from white teachers who questioned her guidance and authority since she was not the principal. One teacher went as far as reporting her to human resources, but that was later dismissed. The feeling of isolation and pressure to perform well underscored a systematic issue within the Magnolia school district. AA attributed the tremendous growth to her placement at the top school, which is unprecedented for a Black leader.

Soon, AA believed that her accomplishments helped people see past her color since her level of expertise proved she knew what she was doing. Before assuming this administrative role, AA faced questions about being a Black leader in her school, highlighting the racial isolation that she would face in the role.

Throughout her year in this school, she faced microaggressions from parents and staff, which led to her meeting with teachers to talk about her hair, style of dress, and even her promptness to help break down stereotypes and assumptions being expressed. She navigated these experiences gracefully, leveraging them as teachable moments about Black culture. AA discussed the many ways she had to navigate implicit biases and stereotypes, many of which stem from Black women being viewed as aggressive when they ask questions or share their thoughts. She could also be seen as outspoken when advocating for herself, teachers, or students until people realized she was being assertive with her requests.

AA worked hard to dispel any perceptions of being an "angry Black woman" when challenging practices and policies that are not in the best interest of students or teachers, particularly those of color. AA began to speak with a trusted mentor to practice or talk through her responses, learning to be more conscious of her tone and word choice so her content would be noticed in the delivery. The adjustment allowed AA to handle situations tactfully, maintaining her style and professionalism. She remained resilient and eventually gained the respect of her peers and superiors in her district while bringing attention to systemic inequities. AA could redefine her identity and overcome the stereotypes that teachers were attempting to place upon her by white teachers and parents within her school setting.

She also talked about having to consistently prove her knowledge, which upholds the systemic issue of varying beliefs about the ability of Black women to do their jobs. In addition to the challenges she faced in her role, AA faced opposition when applying for district-level leadership roles. This resistance is perceived to be related to race, especially since the resistance came mainly from white women. When an executive leadership position in the math department was available and subsequently awarded to a white woman with a literacy background, she knew her expertise was overlooked because of her race. The new appointee relied on AA to support her with content and professional learning for teachers across the district. The experience was jolting, but since then, she has developed a network to resolve her challenges, gain insight, and exchange ideas with present and former colleagues from various schools and districts.

Beyond working to make a positive academic impact, AA also advocates for more diversity and representation within the schools. One example was after a tragedy struck a school; AA recognized that the five white female counselors who were sent to a predominantly Black school to support grieving students would not be a good fit. As a change agent, she immediately let the district know about the disconnect and how students would not be receptive; they needed people of color they could connect with at that moment. She has advocated for change within her school district by highlighting a need across the district to be more cognizant of hiring practices and inclusivity. AA spoke about the lack of equitable hiring practices, but also noted that when Black administrators are hired, they are typically placed in Black or Title I settings, and white administrators are placed in schools with a population that looks like them. The issue of Black leaders rarely being placed in higher-performing schools is something she has talked about with district leaders.

AA compared vice president Kamala Harris's candidacy to her own experiences. She pointed out that even her expertise in a specific role should not determine her readiness for leadership; the collective experiences that have prepared her for the work should be considered. This comparison magnifies the need for fair and inclusive hiring practices.

Dannie's Journey: Coaching While Black in Different School Environments

Dannie knew from a young age that she would become an educator; words from her mom affirmed her leadership abilities. She has worked in education for over twenty years and has spent the last ten years as an instructional coach within Title I and predominantly white settings. Noticing the inequities between the schools she and her siblings attended fueled her desire to advocate for students and equitable learning opportunities regardless of whether they attended a neighborhood or magnet school. Dannie started her career as a pre- K and kindergarten teacher, later becoming an instructional leader and earning an advanced degree. As an instructional coach, she began working with only one grade level, eventually serving a broader range of grade levels and content areas, which stretched her as a leader. Dannie reflected on how being a Black woman significantly impacted her experiences with the willingness of teachers to be receptive, varying based on the school's demographics. Within predominantly Black schools, she was received well. In contrast, in predominantly white schools, teachers were more resistant, less likely to trust her, and often questioned her intellect in favor of their former white instructional coach.

Dannie experienced direct and indirect biases as a Black woman instructional coach, with her intellectual contributions being undervalued despite her wide range of training. Regardless, she aspires to empower teachers to "look within to find solutions rather than doing the work for them" by implementing proven methods that previously yielded high success. Fueled by biases, the resistance hurt her effectiveness in the teachers' role in the classroom. Resistant teachers felt that Dannie was less knowledgeable due to her innate ability to "teach you how to enact a new teaching strategy rather than doing it for the teachers," contrary to their prior experiences with coaching.

Her approach to coaching, which pushed teachers to think more critically and take ownership of their learning, was sometimes perceived as aggressive and insensitive, particularly by her non-Black colleagues. It also includes leveraging data to reinforce coaching goals and provide a concrete source of evidence. In the more rural setting, the staff was more resistant to her coaching; there was less ownership and self-directed accountability to comply with changes she was attempting to implement to the detriment of the school. While in the priority Title I school, the challenge was more connected to the lack of resources (guest speakers, instructional materials, and field trips for exposure), which limited the opportunities for students to have new experiences. The scarcity of resources limited the growth despite being among a more cohesive staff. Regardless of her challenges, she knows the importance of serving as an instructional coach to prepare for future instructional leadership roles beyond the school level.

The biases Dannie has encountered related to race, gender, and age did not stop her pursuit of becoming an instructional leader. However, she noticed they were a barrier to being offered roles that less qualified white colleagues were selected to fill. She emphasized the importance of resilience and remaining focused on best practices while navigating biases that can lead to discouragement. She leverages teacher feedback to measure impact, viewing the growth teachers experience as a marker of her success in her role. Dannie also celebrated her school's progress in her most recent role, moving from the lowest-performing school in the state and making significant gains. To overcome her struggles, Dannie utilized relationship building as her primary strategy. She also engages in strength-based coaching to adapt based on how receptive teachers are to her support and tailors her support to their personality and individual needs. Her adaptability allows her to provide flexibility as she provides feedback to teachers in a manner that they are receptive to implementing changes.

Community plays an important role in helping Dannie navigate challenging situations with her colleagues, friends, and mentors. Her support system was a place of solace, provided her strength, and assisted her in navigating the difficulties she encountered as an instructional coach. Dannie discussed the need to be resilient and remain focused on research and best practices to guide the work, even when she encounter biases or feel discouraged. Dannie talked in depth about how Black women in instructional leadership roles must spend more time proving themselves in spaces that undervalue their work and contributions. She urges Black women to remain focused on their work and push past the barriers and biases to succeed. Her resilience is connected to her ability to manage her stress to avoid burning out in her role. She uses various coping mechanisms such as midday reflections, taking PD regarding crucial conversations, and mindset training. Managing her emotions throughout the day was essential in continuing the work amid resistance.

Ivy's Journey: Overcoming Bias and Advocating for Students

Ivy has worked in education for the past twenty-one years, driven by her passion to help others and make an impact. She envisioned a career where she could continue to help others. After several years as a classroom teacher, she was recruited as a curriculum specialist to support teachers. Within the last five to six years, she transitioned to be an academic coach across the K–12 setting and is now based at a high school. She has often been sought out to take on leadership roles. In her experiences, she feels Black women are in a position where they have to work much harder to be valued and acknowledged in the room. One example is being in a space that is white or male-dominated, where her input is often questioned, dismissed, or fact-checked. This occurs despite the fact that she often has more experience and training than those making the decisions.

Throughout her career, Ivy has encountered challenges with her white colleagues, many of whom aspire to establish themselves as her superiors despite her extensive experience in various roles and her skills. An example she shared was being a Black woman with the most knowledge of any of her leadership team: four male assistant principals, one white female assistant principal, and a white male principal. Her input was often ignored, or she was excluded from conversations about the curriculum. Ivy has observed disparities in the way white women are frequently fast-tracked into administrative roles while Black women are challenged to work much harder or go through extra steps to be considered for the same roles. The unequal treatment has sometimes left her feeling frustrated and isolated.

In her role, Ivy is aware of the oppressive institutional barriers she faces, leading to double standards and being relegated to demeaning roles that do not consider her leadership skills, while assigning her colleagues with less experience more leadership opportunities, underscoring Ivy's awareness of blatant bias. One microaggression is that she is asked to work with or speak to the Black teachers or students who are perceived as challenging within the school. Her experiences include teachers assuming she has shared experiences with Black students due to their identity, often assigning stereotypical similarities, for example, living in poverty, coming from a single- parent home, and being exposed to drugs. Additionally, throughout her career, she has consistently had to work to show she belongs in her role and prove herself after seeing her colleagues overlook and second-guess her work. She has often been perceived as aggressive or angry when she speaks up or calls out unjust treatment. She is mindful of the tone of her inter-

actions to avoid being stereotyped. Ivy has intentionally established rapport with her colleagues to strengthen her relationships
with teachers. She knows this means adapting her approach to lead
with "firmness and grace." Ivy has learned to use data and research to overcome biases and validate the content she shares with
teachers to build her credibility, as more people can see improvement in teacher practice.

In the data meetings, Ivy advocates for the students as the administrative team and teachers meet to identify the disparities,
namely, student discipline. Ivy points out where African American
students receive a disproportionate number of referrals and how
minority students tend to be punished more harshly than their
white peers. She advocates for the equitable treatment of minority
students. Additionally, Ivy talked about how this school has long
had a diverse representation of students in AP courses until recently. She emphasizes the need for more diversity and representation
in those advanced courses and prompts the school guidance counselors to be more actively engaged in addressing this gap. Her
ability to be a voice who speaks up for and represents minority
students is one reason she remains at the school despite her concerns about the lack of racial diversity in leadership and the teaching population.

With minimal support from her district, Ivy draws strength
from her personal network of education leaders. Her network
gives her a space to receive guidance, resources, and encouragement as she navigates the challenges and nuances of her role. The
changes she sees in teacher practice help her see her influence and
how she can be a positive light for others in her district. Ivy finds
strength when leaning on a network of Black women who offer
support and wisdom. Being a part of a community helps to build
her confidence and provides her with encouragement and ways to
be strategic in her work. She now has a space to validate her job

and be reminded of its impact and importance. She has a legacy as the first Black instructional coach, which, within a year, led to two others being hired for the role. She hopes to continue to inspire others to do this work, which is not always easy but has a lasting impact. As a result of her most recent experiences, she has questioned whether she needs to move into a different role. Sadly, her most recent challenges with race and gender have left her considering a move into a new career path. Although she knows her voice as a Black woman instructional coach is needed, she is trying to find her footing as she feels at a dead end in her current role.

Jade's Journey: Defining Leadership and Setting Boundaries

Jade's journey in education spans back to 2009 and is rooted in the positive experiences she has had with mentors who inspired her to be an educator. After being a classroom teacher, she transitioned to working with new teachers and co-teaching to support instruction, later becoming a math facilitator. This new role allowed her to support planning to ensure the curriculum was aligned with the standards, leading data chats, pulling small groups, and modeling in classrooms as needed. She has served as an instructional coach for about seven years, and her formal and informal experiences have given her a range of expertise. She attributes her success in her role to her focus on building community and creating a village with support as her primary means of relationship building with teachers. She believes that her cultural background has influenced her ability to cultivate a nurturing environment where teachers and her colleagues feel comfortable requesting support due to the level of trust that has been established.

Working in an instructional coaching role is important for becoming an effective school leader. While in the role, she observed that her white and male counterparts have been able to advance into administrative roles and beyond the classroom; they did not have to work within a coaching role. Although this is true, Jade feels the coaching role is essential since an administrator needs to be instructionally sound and savvy enough to support and potentially coach teachers. Working as a math and science instructional coach, she often encounters people who are surprised she is in the role since those subjects are typically male-dominated. Some of the biases she has endured were related to race and gender. As a Black woman thriving in her role, she found herself trying to gain the trust of more experienced teachers, especially if they were not African American. Many times, she had to prove her expertise to overcome the biases. Alternatively, she shared that her white colleagues did not experience the same level of scrutiny or skepticism, nor did they ever share feelings of the need to prove or validate themselves to the teachers they served.

Jade has faced challenges with her supervisor, a Black woman, who has provided unequal treatment in comparison to her white colleagues regarding their tasks or demands. For example, Jade was unexpectedly asked to leave her duties in the classroom to conduct a learning walk. She knew this was a request that would not have been made of her white counterpart since her colleague would speak up and oppose the request. Sometimes, she has been called "angry or difficult" due to the direct way she delivers her coaching, while colleagues in similar situations have been met with sympathy. Jade talked about experiencing doubt from teachers since the bulk of her experience was in the Title I setting. Her primary challenge was that teachers saw her skills as less adaptable to meet the needs of a more affluent population, which built a level of resistance in establishing her credibility within her role. Aside from student performance, Jade reflects on the growth she observes in teachers over time when thinking about measuring impact. She discussed seeing a teacher move from being reluctant to speak up to taking on leadership roles. Jade also advocates for the diverse needs of students in the school setting, for example, English language learners (ELs) and students with Individualized Education Plans (IEPs). There have been many instances where she has had to speak up against the tendency to segregate students based on their performance abilities. The structure leaves lower-level students in classes together, but the higher-performing students need more opportunities to advance due to a lack of peer-to-peer challenges. Jade has played a role in organizing heritage-based programs to celebrate the diverse populations represented in the school. She has often felt compelled to speak up when she notices disparities in expectations for students of color. She aspires to create a school culture that authentically supports students' academic and personal growth.

Jade has discussed the importance of having a "Black girl tribe," a supportive network of Black women educators and instructional leaders with whom she can share her challenges and receive advice for the next steps. She hopes to inspire other Black women in education to pursue leadership roles. She is committed to mentoring young teachers, especially those from HBCUs, while encouraging them to take on leadership tasks and roles in their journey.

Phalan's Journey: Relationship Building as a Survival Tool

Phalan is an educator with over twenty years of experience as an instructional coach. She could share various experiences that she felt were influenced by her race and gender. Throughout her twenty-year career, she has worked in affluent and Title I schools; she prefers working in the Title I setting as it resonates with her childhood experiences. As a child, Phalan had several people who influenced her, but she felt her experiences with poverty were a big motivator for her. In middle school, one teacher was also a church member who served as a role model. She wanted to have the impact on others that her middle school teacher had on her. As Phalan shared her journey as an instructional coach, I noticed it was more diverse and rapid than that of others. After two years in the classroom, she quickly became a literacy facilitator when the district had to approve this request, especially since she had not taught for long.

She emphasizes leveraging relationship building to counter the biases and challenges encountered as a Black woman in an instructional coaching role. She talks about how building rapport has served her well, countering biases and helping to establish a "foundation of mutual respect." As she reflected on the various challenges she has encountered in predominantly white schools compared to those in high-poverty or predominantly Black schools, she saw the resistance come in the form of questioning her expertise, leading to her having to prove herself. Conversely, in high-poverty settings, she finds resistance from white teachers who display pity for Black students and, therefore, find it difficult to align with her high expectations for all learners. As an instructional coach, Phalan often feels she has had to prove her competence and knowledge. Many times, Phalan has felt as though she needed to go above and beyond just to be considered an equal to her white counterparts. Her principal was selecting one distinct memory, and Phalan had to join her at a low-performing school. Phalan discussed instances where teachers would leave planning sessions to complain about them to the principal, which felt like they were challenging her leadership. This was ongoing, but the principal's support seemed to lessen early in her career. Phalan also noticed that as her confidence grew in her content, those challenges lessened in some ways. Phalan has relied on using the "sandwich" approach when giving feedback, allowing her to deliver critical feedback in a way that was well received by those resistant to change in their practice. An advantage of having experience in multiple settings has allowed her to be flexible in her role and approach to coaching teachers. She has learned to choose her battles and reserve her energy for addressing situations directly impacting students. With another leader, Phalan experienced a turning point in her career. When her principal came down hard on the team instead of offering her support, she expected Phalan to be OK while asking her if her white colleagues "were OK and were likely to come into work the next day?" For Phalan, this underscored that even Black women in leadership might not be allies for their people.

The main way Phalan has advocated is by sharing strength-based thinking for teachers, getting them to raise their expectations for their students. By asking teachers to teach to the rigor or the standards while providing appropriate scaffolds, she aims to counter the narrative that builds on the educational inequities that minority students experience. During Hispanic Heritage Month, she led the establishment of a program for the school; she learned this was the first time in the school's history that they celebrated this culture. This was an opportunity to celebrate the heritage of the students and community stakeholders to break barriers within the school.

Phalan believes there is value in observing the positive changes in school climate and culture and that success should be measured beyond the quantitative. She can see a shift in teacher practices as she reflects on her impact. She aims to influence other instructional coaches and educators by building a legacy to create a space for educational equity and student achievement.

Michelle's Journey: Advocacy, Representation, and Navigating Bias

Michelle was inspired to become an educator because she came from a family of educators and ministers; she felt this was part of her identity. Her educational journey began as a Career Technical

Education (CTE) business teacher. Eventually, she moved into an official role as an instructional coach, leading her to serve as a classroom teacher, team lead, department chair, and instructional coach over the past twenty-two years. Michelle feels, as a Black woman, she has been able to represent strength, leadership, and hope to those she serves despite encountering stereotypes of being labeled as "intimidating or unapproachable." Michelle discussed remaining at her first school for twenty years to provide representation for students with a similar background. This underscores her commitment to being an advocate and her resilience as she later reflected on the toxic nature of that environment.

Despite being overqualified, she identified how her race and gender caused challenges in her journey, and she often saw those less qualified or with less experience being promoted at a much faster rate, some even being promoted to administrative roles while still enrolled in an educational leadership program. She recalled one specific instance when she applied for a role as an administrator, but when told she didn't get the role, they cited it was because they were not hiring internally; later, she saw an internal candidate was indeed promoted for the role. She faced implicit biases, which included colleagues questioning her expertise and undervaluing her work and contributions compared to her non-Black colleagues, making it difficult for her to establish herself as a credible instructional leader. Michelle has a direct leadership style, which has led to instances where her contributions are overlooked or dismissed in a meeting, while a white woman could present the same idea, and her idea would be embraced. When encountering resistance, Michelle has learned to adapt her support for teachers based on the needs, experience, and receptiveness of the teacher(s) she is coaching. Relationship building has been a bridge to building trust and positive change in her environment.

Michelle established clear boundaries to protect her mental health to ensure she could be more effective in her role. She has learned to "choose her battles" when deciding which microaggressions and biases she encounters and what to address.

Community is one strategy Michelle leveraged to build resiliency and navigate the challenges she faces. She gains strength from her community and personal network, her "treasure box" of mentors, allowing her to overcome tough instances or challenges. Her current principal, a Black woman, is a thought partner who values her input and pushes her to go after her goals. Michelle has developed a program called Teach, Learn, Inspire, which focuses on teacher collaboration and student progress, a tool she will use to measure impact and discuss the findings with her current administrator. Her relationship with this administrator is a stark contrast to her previous encounters.

Her advocacy work has led her to be a voice, creating space for conversations to develop a more inclusive school environment. She worked as a coach and created spaces for students to gather in clubs or after school, so they had a point of contact with an instructional leader of color. Serving as the only Black leader provided a way to give students a point of connectivity. Michelle discussed collaborating with a colleague to bring the first Black History program in over two decades, stamping the need for representation. She remained in her role despite feeling she was consistently overlooked and treated more as an outsider than an instructional coach, which she mainly attributes to her identity as a Black woman serving with a predominantly white leadership team.

Her story is one of endurance and vision. She carried the emotional labor of her role with grace, believing deeply in the power of representation and community.

You've just read several real-life stories, unfiltered, layered, and full of struggle and strength. The HERStories in this chapter are not just reflections of individual experiences. They're patterns. They're truths. They also reveal a clear need for a coaching model that speaks to the realities of Black women in these roles. What follows is not a how-to guide built on theory alone. It's grounded in the lived experiences you've just read. It's built from the themes that surfaced in their words: resilience, resistance, advocacy, and the need to redefine leadership in a system that wasn't built with us in mind.

The next chapter introduces you to the NURTURE model: a coaching framework created to affirm, guide, and sustain BWICs. From naming lived experiences to elevating your career, each component supports your growth while honoring who you are and how you lead.

This is where strategy meets soul. Let's begin.

II

Part Two:
The Path Forward

CHAPTER 3

The NURTURE Model

The HERStories shared in the previous chapter reveal not only the realities BWICs face but also the urgency of our leadership. While the participants in this study shared unique experiences, what emerged from their stories were shared themes of challenge, identity, and power. These themes became the foundation of the NURTURE model, a coaching framework designed to affirm the lived realities of BWICs while offering a path forward.

This model is not meant to replace existing coaching practices that are working well. Instead, it provides a culturally sustaining lens that centers on the needs and experiences of Black women. The NURTURE model is grounded in research, experience, and reflection. It acknowledges how BWICs are often unseen, offering tools to help them lead, sustain, and thrive in their roles.

The **NURTURE model** is a framework designed to help BWICs do more than survive in these spaces. It equips them to lead gracefully, influence their environments, and drive systemic change at the district and school levels.

N – Name and Nurture Lived Experiences and Expertise

The first step in this model is naming and nurturing. Too often, Black women coaches are expected to show up with strength while minimizing their own stories. Their lived experiences are rarely validated in professional settings, yet those experiences are part of what makes their leadership so impactful.

BWICs bring layers of personal and professional insight to their roles. This insight is shaped by how they've been taught, treated, and tested. It is an essential part of how they coach. Rather than separating personal experience from professional contribution, the NURTURE model urges BWICs to embrace and name both.

Naming your lived experience doesn't mean turning every moment into a coaching story. It means allowing your past to inform your present and resisting the pressure to leave parts of yourself behind to be accepted. It also means recognizing and celebrating your expertise. You are not just someone who "supports." You are someone who leads, develops, and transforms. You are an instructional leader with a powerful, needed, and valuable perspective. Nurturing yourself means slowing down enough to reflect. It means permitting yourself to rest, learn, and trust what you already know. You don't need to earn belonging. You already belong.

Self-Coaching Reflection

- Where do I feel pressure to tone down my personality or leadership style?
- How can I bring my full self to coaching without fear?

Take a moment to reflect.

Now, let's go deeper.

BWICs should not have to choose between being effective and being acceptable. Yet, many participants in my study shared how often their passion, conviction, or directness was misread. Their confidence was perceived as aggression. Their clarity was labeled as combative. This misinterpretation forced them to constantly assess how they showed up in professional spaces.

Dannie, one of the instructional coaches in my study, described her approach as "teaching teachers how to fish." She didn't just offer answers—she developed capacity. Her focus was on long-term growth, not short-term compliance. Even with her clear commitment to supporting teachers, she encountered pushback from those uncomfortable with her leadership. But she did not shrink. She stayed grounded in her coaching philosophy and found ways to adjust her delivery without silencing her voice.

Coaching Strategy

To navigate these challenges, it's important to establish a clear coaching identity that reflects your expertise and authenticity. A powerful first step is creating your coaching identity statement. This statement serves as a compass, guiding how you lead, advocate, and show up fully in your work.

Reflect on the following:

- What coaching frameworks or philosophies guide your practice?
- How does your identity inform your coaching approach?
- Why is it important for you to show up as your full self in this work?

By naming and owning your coaching identity, you can move with clarity, build trust, and sustain your work without compromising who you are.

Call to Action

Draft your coaching identity statement.

Start with a few sentences that capture how you coach, what matters to you, and how your identity shapes your leadership. This isn't just a personal exercise—it's a declaration.

Tape it to your wall. Revisit it often.

Let it remind you that your voice, presence, and practice are not just necessary but essential.

U – Unify & Build Collaborative Relationships

Coaching cannot thrive in isolation. One of the most powerful tools BWICs carry is the ability to build meaningful relationships. This work is grounded in trust. And while relationship building is often expected, it's rarely supported in tangible ways.

This model component calls for intentional collaboration, not just with teachers, but with other leaders. Unifying doesn't mean agreeing on everything. It means identifying shared goals and building from a place of mutual respect and clarity.

Coaching is not just about strategy. It's about trust.

Phalan, an instructional coach with over twenty-two years of experience, emphasized this beautifully when she said, "It all begins with relationships. Bias starts to melt away when people see you as a person first." When relationships are strong, resistance softens. Biases begin to fade. And trust becomes the foundation for meaningful growth.

Self-Coaching Reflection

- How do I currently build trust in my coaching relationships?
- Where do I struggle to establish credibility?

To build trust, coaches must show up with authenticity, consistency, and care. Teachers are far more likely to be open and reflective when they trust their coach to support their growth without judgment. Once trust is broken, it's difficult to repair—so relationship building must be a deliberate, ongoing part of your practice.

Sometimes, that's as simple as pausing to connect before jumping into business. A quick check-in before a planning session can remind teachers that you see them—not just their data. Asking about their goals, acknowledging their progress, or expressing genuine interest in their journey can create a culture of mutual respect and receptiveness.

Trust is also built through credibility. For Black women coaches, credibility is often unfairly questioned, which makes it even more critical to be clear, confident, and prepared. Storytelling and data can help reinforce your expertise.

Reflect on how you frame your coaching identity:

- What instructional strategies have worked for you—and why?
- How have you helped teachers grow and succeed?

What evidence (data, outcomes, testimonials) supports your approach?

When faced with skepticism, lean into what you know. Use your experience, your voice, and your results to anchor the conversation in truth.

Coaching Strategy: Develop Coaching Conversation Starters

Coaching conversations are most effective when they invite reflection—not resistance. When teachers express limiting beliefs, respond with strategic questions that prompt deeper thinking.

For example:

If a teacher says, "These students are unmotivated[EM1] ," consider: "Tell me about a time they surprised you with their engagement. What made that moment different?"

If a teacher says, "They just can't handle this work, reframe with:

"Which skill have they mastered recently? How can we bridge that to this new challenge?"

These types of questions redirect focus to potential, not problems.

Call to Action

Choose one new trust-building move to implement this week. That could be a check-in before a coaching session, a shift in how you acknowledge a teacher's strengths, or a new strategy for navigating resistance.

Consider:

What will this approach look, feel, and sound like in practice?

Then try it—and reflect on what changed.

Building trust takes time, but consistent, intentional steps will deepen your relationships and expand your influence as a coach and a leader.

R – Reflect & Refine Your Coaching Practice

Reflection is foundational to strong coaching. For BWICs, that reflection must also include the invisible labor we often carry. Are you adjusting your tone because someone once said you were "too direct"? Are you over- preparing because you've been questioned before? Are you holding back in meetings to avoid being labeled?

These reflections aren't signs of insecurity. They're signs of awareness. But awareness alone is not enough. We must be intentional about what we do with the insights we gain.

Refining your coaching practice means grounding your strategies in both research and lived experience. It means asking, "Is my approach based on who I truly am—or who I think I need to be to fit in?" It means using your coaching voice with clarity, even when others resist it. This section invites BWICs to reflect honestly and refine their practice with confidence. You do not need to coach like someone else to be effective. You need to coach from your strengths, with purpose and authenticity.

I remember the pressure I felt when I moved from coaching K–2 math to coaching K–5 literacy. I believed I needed to master every element of literacy instruction immediately. The weight of needing to prove myself felt heavy. But I eventually realized that being a leader is not about knowing everything. It's about staying committed to growth. I could coach with more confidence and clarity when I stopped focusing on what I lacked and started building on what I brought.

Self-Coaching Reflection Questions

- What are three coaching skills I excel in?
- Where do I feel uncertain, and why?

Knowing your strengths matters. Confidence in your abilities helps you stand firm when your expertise is questioned. Many Black women in coaching roles are repeatedly asked to prove themselves. This makes it even more important to clearly identify what you do well.

There is also strength in knowing where you need to grow. When you name your areas for development, you can seek support through professional learning, mentorship, or collaboration. Growth is not a sign of weakness. It is a leadership choice.

Call to Action

Complete a strength-based coaching self-assessment. Identify where you feel most confident and where you want to improve. Choose one specific area of growth and create a plan to develop that skill. This might include reading professional texts, engaging in targeted PD, or seeking feedback from a trusted mentor.

Refining your coaching practice is not about fixing what's broken. It's about owning your growth and honoring your journey.

T – Transform Mindsets & School Culture

BWICs are often asked to drive change without the support to transform the mindsets and systems that block it. This part of the model centers the coach as a culture shifter, moving strategically, intentionally, and with an equity-driven purpose.

Transformation requires courage. It means disrupting deficit narratives about students, challenging low expectations, and asking difficult questions about access, placement, and discipline. It also means shifting how others perceive Black women coaches—not as helpers or fixers, but as instructional leaders with expertise and authority.

Too often, BWICs are hired into roles with limited decision-making power. They are tasked with "supporting" teachers but are excluded from leadership decisions. This limits their impact and sends a message that their voice is optional.

Jalen, a highly qualified instructional coach, experienced this firsthand. Her expertise was regularly questioned or dismissed.

She was overlooked by leaders, resisted by teachers, and undervalued in spaces where she should have been seen. Despite her accomplishments, she began to doubt herself. She hesitated to assert her authority, even when she knew she had the knowledge and skills to lead. Eventually, Jalen realized she did not need to keep proving her worth. She needed to own it.

Transforming culture begins with how you carry yourself, but it must be matched by how others recognize and respond to your leadership. For school and district leaders reading this, the culture shift you want cannot happen without examining how power is shared. BWICs cannot shift mindsets alone. But with strategic allies, clear boundaries, and a strong focus on students, they can begin to reshape what is possible.

Self-Coaching Reflection Questions

- When do I feel the need to overexplain or prove myself?
- What internal beliefs must I unlearn to fully step into my leadership?
- How does my coaching presence shift when I feel confident versus uncertain?

Coaching is not only about improving instruction. It is about challenging mindsets. That includes the mindsets of the teachers we support and our beliefs about ourselves.

We are not coaching a problem. We are coaching a person. That means we must be willing to address the assumptions and biases that shape how teachers view students, instruction, and even our role.

Many teachers enter the profession holding deficit-based beliefs about Black and Brown students. When those beliefs go unchallenged, teachers focus on what students lack instead of what they bring. BWICs are often called on to fix struggling students or teachers without being positioned as true partners in improving instructional quality for all learners. This is why coaching for mindset shifts is critical.

Coaching Strategy: Reframing Deficit Thinking

When you hear deficit-based language, consider how you might reframe the conversation with strength-based questioning.

If a teacher says, "These students just don't care about learning," you might respond with:

"What is something your students have been excited about lately? Let's build on that."

If a teacher says, "They just don't have the skills to succeed," try: "Where have they already shown progress? Let's start there."

The goal is not to call teachers out. It is to call them into reflection. Your questions can become a mirror, helping them see their students through a new lens.

Call to Action

Transformation begins within. Start by identifying one limiting belief you have internalized about yourself as a Black woman instructional coach. Then, develop a personal strategy to unlearn it.

Next, identify a teacher who holds a deficit-based mindset. Plan a coaching conversation that guides them toward a more asset-based perspective.

The first step to thriving in your role is transforming how you see yourself. The next step is influencing how others see you and how they see the students you serve.

Your voice, your expertise, and your presence matter. Stand in that truth.

U – Uplift & Advocate for Educators

Advocacy is more than a passion. For many BWICs, it is a necessity. They see the gaps in access, the disparities in outcomes, and the absence of representation across leadership roles. And they step in.

This part of the model centers advocacy as a core component of coaching. It invites BWICs to use their voices to make suggestions in PLCs and influence policies, practices, and decisions that center on equity. It is about using your platform to push conversations forward, and it requires owning your expertise, without apology.

Despite years of experience and deep instructional knowledge, many BWICs are asked to prove their value in ways their counterparts are not. Owning your expertise and using data to showcase your impact helps shift perceptions and ensures your role is seen and respected.

Uplifting others also means recognizing that your presence alone changes the dynamic. When you speak up, question norms, or name patterns that others ignore, you are advocating. You are building capacity when you mentor a newer coach or encourage a teacher to step into leadership. You are challenging a system that does not always welcome change, and your advocacy plants the seeds for something better.

Consider the example of Mrs. Phillips, a teacher I coached. In our early sessions, her lessons lacked alignment with grade-level standards. But over time, she began to embrace new strategies. As her confidence grew, so did her students' performance, increasing from 40 percent to 70 percent proficiency. The transformation was not only instructional. It was a shift in mindset, expectations, and belief in what was possible. That is the power of advocacy in action.

It is also important to remember that advocacy does not have to be loud to be effective. Some advocate by speaking up in meetings. Others influence quietly through behind-the-scenes leadership. Both are valid. What matters most is staying grounded in your purpose and understanding the value of your presence.

Self-Coaching Reflection Questions

- How do I currently measure and share my impact?
- Where do I need to advocate for myself more often?

Coaching Strategy: Turning Data into a Story & Advocating for Yourself

One of the most powerful things you can do as a coach is learn how to turn your data into a compelling story. When paired with intentional advocacy, it becomes a way to elevate your voice and position your work as essential.

Start with small wins. Use early successes to build momentum and credibility.

Leverage data to validate your expertise. Highlight measurable growth in teacher practice or student learning.

Use coaching placements strategically. Work with engaged teachers first and let their results become a model for others.

At the same time, reflect on where you might need to speak up more whether about your responsibilities, boundaries, or the support needed to do your job well. Many BWICs do incredible work that goes unrecognized. Advocating for yourself ensures that your leadership is acknowledged and sustained.

Call to Action

This quarter, share one data-driven coaching success with your administrator. Use real metrics, teacher growth, or student outcomes to highlight your contribution. Present it clearly and confidently. Framing your impact in this way helps others understand the depth of your work and reinforces the need for continued support.

By owning your expertise, using data to tell your story, and advocating for your role, you position yourself not just as a coach—but as a leader with influence.

R – Resilience in Leadership

Resilience is a critical skill for BWICs. It sustains you through the nuance of leadership, the emotional labor of advocacy, and the unspoken expectations that often accompany your role. As a coach, you're not only responsible for supporting instruction—you're also navigating complex systems, pushing for equity, and holding space for both your students and colleagues. These responsibilities, while meaningful, can take a toll.

This section focuses on the intentional work required to preserve your energy, protect your peace, and lead without burning out. It is about understanding that your capacity is not unlimited and that setting boundaries is not selfish—it is necessary.

Too often, BWICs are expected to do more, know more, and be more without ever asking for more. Continuously justifying your leadership, proving your impact, or representing every marginalized voice in the building can be exhausting. Developing resilience in all areas of your life helps you sustain your leadership with clarity, care, and purpose.

Self-Coaching Reflection Questions

- Where do I currently feel the most strain in my coaching role?

- What boundaries do I need to establish to sustain my leadership?

As you reflect on where your energy is being drained, consider how you might make space for what replenishes you. Below are a few strategies to guide your practice:

- **Prioritize rest**. You cannot pour into others if you are depleted. Make rest and recovery a part of your leadership rhythm.

- **Set and hold your boundaries**. Define your work hours. Clarify your role. Say no when you need to. Boundaries protect your leadership.

- **Build your community**. Resilience is not about going it alone. Surround yourself with people who pour into you, offer wisdom, and remind you of your purpose.

- **Stay asset-minded**. In difficult moments, lean on your strengths and your team's strengths.

Coaching Strategy: Leadership Sustainability Plan

To lead with resilience, you need a personal sustainability plan. This is not about doing more. It's about protecting what matters most.

- Choose one boundary to reinforce.
- Identify one support system to lean into.
- Commit to one renewal practice to sustain your leadership.

Whether it's taking Friday evenings off, joining a monthly check-in with fellow BWICs, or setting time aside each week for learning, your plan should work for you.

Call to Action

What's one habit or practice you can implement this month to support your leadership resilience? Write it down. Name it. Commit to it.

Your well-being is not optional. It's essential to your impact, growth, and longevity in this work.

E – Elevate Your Impact & Influence

Your instructional coaching and leadership role go beyond the day-to-day; it's about the path you create for yourself and those who come after you. As a Black woman instructional coach, your impact stretches beyond guiding teachers. You are shaping the future of education and opening doors for future Black leaders.

It's time to think about what's next. Maybe you've thought about moving into a district-level or administrative role. Perhaps you're considering becoming a consultant or stepping into executive leadership. The transition from coach to leader at the next level is not only about skill; it's about support. Consider the people who have helped you get to this point. Who mentored you? Who helped you navigate new spaces? Their support likely shaped your journey, and now it's your turn to be intentional about how you mentor others.

Growth is not just about building your network. It's also about paying it forward. Mentorship sustains leadership. Whether seeking a mentor or becoming one, your influence grows when you allow others to rise.

Self-Coaching Reflection Questions

- What leadership roles interest me beyond coaching?
- Who are my mentors, and how can I build my leadership network?

Coaching Strategies

Mentorship Mapping

Identifying the right mentors is a key step in growing your leadership. Reflect on who in your network can offer guidance, insight, or open doors. Think about those who have successfully moved into the spaces you want to enter. If you don't have a mentor, whom could you contact? Find someone whose values and path align with your professional goals.

Leadership Branding Exercise

Your leadership brand is how others perceive you, your expertise, presence, and impact. Consider how you show up in meetings, coaching conversations, and professional spaces. Are you confident in your voice and leadership, or are you holding back? What small shifts can you make now to begin positioning yourself for your next level? That might mean seeking targeted professional development, speaking up strategically, or taking on a leadership role within your current position.

Creating Your Leadership Road Map

Leadership doesn't happen by accident; it requires strategy. Begin mapping out where you want to be in the next three to five years. Think about the roles you're drawn to, the skills you want to sharpen, and the opportunities you need to pursue. A road map helps clarify your direction and reminds you that growth is intentional.

Call to Action

Outline your five-year leadership vision. Where do you want to be, and what steps will help you get there? Identify one mentor to reach out to, one leadership move to make this quarter, and one skill you'll focus on refining. Your leadership journey doesn't begin when you get a new title; it starts now, with your work and how you show up in it. Own it.

Conclusion: Flourish as a Leader and Change Agent

This framework is designed to help you step fully into your leadership, navigate resistance confidently, and create lasting change without burning out or shrinking yourself.

Surviving is the starting point; transformation is the goal.

The NURTURE model is more than a coaching framework. It is a leadership strategy designed to empower BWICs.

Now that you understand the NURTURE framework, the next step is bringing it to life in your coaching practice. This book is not just about theory; it is a coaching companion meant to help you implement strategies, reflect on your practice, and strengthen your leadership.

Building a Nurture Coaching Practice in Your School

When I first stepped into my role as a district-level instructional coach responsible for coaching other coaches, I felt an overwhelming need for all the answers. I believed I had to master every coaching move and anticipate every possible challenge. But when I paused to reflect on my training and experience, I reminded myself that coaching is not about control. It is about influence. The most impactful coaches do not dictate; they guide, support, and empower. That realization became the foundation of the NURTURE framework and the approach I use to build a sustainable and effective coaching practice.

This chapter explores how to apply the NURTURE model in your day-to-day coaching. Whether you are facilitating professional development, leading PLCs, or coaching one-on-one,

NURTURE offers a mindset and strategy, not just a checklist. Look at each component and consider how it can shape your work.

N – Name & Nurture Lived Experiences & Expertise

Your identity as a coach shapes how you support teachers. Authenticity is essential. Teachers, like students, respond best to realness. As a Black woman instructional coach, I've walked into schools where my authority was questioned before I even introduced myself. The pressure to prove myself was constant.

Rather than shrinking to meet expectations, I learned to ask: How do I model authenticity while coaching? What boundaries protect my energy? Bring your full identity into the coaching space and honor the identities of those you support.

U – Unify & Build Collaborative Relationships

Relationships are at the heart of effective coaching. Some teachers will embrace collaboration; others will resist. When you face resistance, pause. Ask yourself: Is this resistance about me—or about the discomfort that comes with change?

Focus on influence rather than control. Build trust and credibility consistently. If your school leadership doesn't fully embrace coaching, find small ways to showcase your impact. Share stories of teacher growth and use data to elevate the value of your work.

R – Reflect & Refine Your Coaching Practice

Imposter syndrome doesn't always go away, it often evolves with new roles and responsibilities. I remember stepping into a district-level coaching position, supporting a learning community of 29 schools. I was the only Black woman in my role and the newest coach on the team. For a moment, I questioned whether my voice would carry the same weight or if I truly fit in that space. But once I began the work, I realized I was exactly where I needed to be. I wasn't there to know everything. I was there to lead with integrity, grow through the process, and bring a perspective that mattered.

Reflect intentionally. Track your wins. Focus on your strengths, and be honest about where you want to grow. Reframe challenges as learning opportunities, not failures. This mindset shift will help you lead with more clarity and confidence.

T – Transform Mindsets & School Culture

Coaching isn't just about supporting teachers—it's about challenging norms that block progress. Whether it's calling out inequitable discipline practices or raising concerns about access to rigorous coursework, your voice matters. You also shift culture by modeling strong leadership. Ask yourself: How do

I feel about my role as an instructional coach? Where do I thrive, and where do I still hold back? Use those reflections to shape your approach and coach with purpose. Helping teachers reframe deficit thinking is part of the work. When a teacher says, "These students just won't engage," help them look at what their students are doing well. Strength-based questions foster growth.

U – Uplift & Advocate for Educators

BWICs are often called on to speak up for equity, whether or not it's in our job description. Use your voice strategically. You don't have to fix everything, but you can push for meaningful change.

If your school has data showing disparities in discipline or achievement, use it to start conversations. When working with teachers, share their progress to show what's possible. Advocacy also means mentoring others and recognizing the importance of your presence.

R – Resilience in Leadership

Resilient coaches don't just survive; they thrive. That means protecting your energy, building community, and leading with confidence. Rest, boundaries, and joy matter.

Ashlee, a coach in a district that didn't value her expertise, leaned on her network to stay grounded. By sharing her impact and using her voice, she sustained her leadership and inspired others. That's resilience in action.

E – Elevate Your Impact & Influence

You are more than your current role. Coaching is a powerful path toward broader leadership. Think about what's next. Maybe you want to move into administration or take on a district leadership role. Who is helping you get there?

Build your network. Find mentors and become one. Own your leadership brand. Think about how you show up in meetings, in classrooms, and in your school community. You are already leading. Step into it with intention.

Applying NURTURE in Different School Cultures

Every school culture is different, and applying NURTURE requires adaptability. Your first goal is to establish credibility in schools with no formal coaching structure. Build strong relationships, highlight teacher growth, and use data to demonstrate the value of coaching. If you're in a school where teachers resist coaching, lead with reflection. Ask thoughtful questions that help teachers challenge their assumptions without feeling attacked. In schools where you advocate for equity, you should lean on data rather than emotion. Document disparities, build a compelling narrative, and push for systemic shifts without carrying the burden of fixing everything on your own.

Making NURTURE Sustainable

To implement NURTURE sustainably, focus on building systems that protect your energy and amplify your impact. Create a coaching schedule that balances planning, conversations, and administrative responsibilities. Track small wins to stay encouraged and document the progress of your work. Most importantly, personal routines should be developed to help prevent burnout. This might include self-care practices, time for reflection, or support from a trusted network. Resilience and sustainability go hand in hand.

Call to Action

Reflect on your school culture. How does it impact your coaching practice? Where can you begin applying NURTURE? Use the 30-Day NURTURE Coaching Challenge in the back of this book to begin integrating small, intentional actions into your daily work. Even if you apply just one strategy per week rather than daily, the reflections will help you stay aligned with your identity, preserve your well-being, and grow as a leader.

Use the weekly coaching reflection templates to track your strengths, growth areas, and small wins. While your strengths and challenges may not shift dramatically weekly, documenting your progress ensures you continue recognizing your impact.

Coaching is a journey, not a checklist. Success doesn't happen overnight, but consistently applying the NURTURE framework will lead to meaningful and lasting change. As you continue this work, remember: You are not just coaching teachers. You are shaping the future of education.

CHAPTER 4

Building a Sustainable Coaching Journey

Coaching is about building trust, offering support, and positively impacting teacher practice. But as a Black woman instructional coach, it's also about navigating unspoken microaggressions, the polite yet formal dismissal of your expertise, and being included in conversations about diversity while excluded from real instructional decision-making.

The exhaustion of being asked to fix inequities—without being given the authority to change the systems that create them—is a reality. For Black women, resistance doesn't just come from teachers. It is often embedded in the very structure of the system itself.

Recognizing Systemic Resistance

Resistance shows up in various ways:

- Tokenism: Being included for optics but excluded from meaningful decisions.
- Disempowerment: Being tasked with student behavior issues but left out of instructional planning.
- Microaggressions: Being spoken over or dismissed in meetings.

- Bias in Leadership: Watching white coaches receive automatic buy-in while you are constantly asked to prove yourself.

This chapter isn't just about navigating these dynamics—it's about knowing when to push, when to pivot, and how to preserve yourself in spaces that weren't built for your thriving.

Understanding Teacher Resistance

Resistance is layered and should not always be treated the same. While some of it is rooted in bias, other forms stem from fear of change or discomfort with new practices. Our role, both unfortunately and powerfully, is to assess the type of resistance we're facing before deciding how to respond.

When Resistance Is About Change

Resistance rooted in discomfort often sounds like:

- "I've always done it this way."
- "This feels like extra work."
- "Why do I have to do this? My students can't handle it."

In these moments, frame changes as manageable and purposeful. Provide specific examples, model the strategy, and use data to create urgency. Showing how student outcomes are tied to instructional shifts can soften resistance and increase buy-in.

When Resistance Is About You

When the resistance feels personal:

- "I don't need this."
- "Why do we have a coach?"
- "I'm just going to talk to admin."

Document these instances and escalate when necessary. If a teacher refuses coaching altogether, redirect the conversation to student outcomes and the larger instructional goals. Don't overexplain yourself—stand firm in your purpose and move the work forward.

Coaching Challenges vs Structural Barriers

Not every issue is a coaching problem. Some challenges are systemic, and you can't fix them with a new strategy. You need to discern what's worth your energy.

When admin doesn't support you: Sometimes the real issue isn't the teacher—it's the way your role is positioned. Ask yourself:

- How was my role introduced?
- Am I empowered to make decisions or only asked to execute them?

Look out for:

- Leaders who reroute teachers to white coaches for "real" instructional support.
- Coaching decisions happening without your voice.
- Praise without power.
- No accountability measures for coaching participation.

Advocating for Your Role

To prevent burnout, advocate for a coaching role that is sustainable and aligned with your expertise.

- Reposition Your Work: If you're often pulled only for equity-related issues, reinforce that equity is foundational to all instruction—not a siloed task.

- Align to School Goals: Show how your work supports school improvement plans.
- Restructure Your Schedule: If administrative tasks consume your time, propose a coaching schedule that prioritizes impact.
- Use Data to Reinforce Value: Highlight teacher growth and student progress tied to your coaching.
- Increase Visibility: Speak in staff meetings. Share wins. Make your work known.

Navigating Microaggressions in Coaching

The challenge isn't just knowing how to respond—it's protecting your peace while doing so. Below are common microaggressions you may face and how you might address them:

- Dismissed or Spoken Over in Meetings: "Yes, I just shared that. How can we build on this idea?"
- Expected to Fix Every Equity Issue: "Equity is a shared responsibility. I'm open to collaborating, but we need collective leadership."
- Tone Policing: "I'm passionate about student success and lead with both strategy and empathy."
- Questioning Your Competence: "Yes. I'm happy to share how this strategy has been effective in similar classrooms."
- Excluded from Decision-Making but Expected to Execute: "Before finalizing this, I'd like to offer input from a coaching lens."
- Skepticism About Your Strategies: "This approach is grounded in research and has proven effective. Let's try it, measure impact, and adjust if needed."

- Being Asked, What Do You Even Do?: "My role is to support teachers in refining their practice to elevate student learning. Let me share a recent success story."

Strategic Responses to Resistance

Not every offense warrants your energy, but every challenge deserves a strategy. Document patterns, set emotional boundaries, and center your coaching goals.

This section includes:

- A Resistance Response Framework
- Tips for Leveraging Data with Leadership
- A Self-Advocacy Plan for Navigating Bias

Resistance doesn't mean stop. It means to strategize. Know when to engage, when to pivot, and when to let your results do the talking. You were hired for a reason. Own your brilliance, protect your peace, and lead boldly.

Expanding Your Leadership and Building Your Support Network

For many of us, coaching was never meant to be the final destination. It was our first step into instructional leadership—a bridge toward broader impact and opportunity. Still, as BWICs, the path forward isn't always clear or accessible. We're often expected to stay in supporting roles, not strategic ones. The truth is: You don't have to wait to be chosen. You can choose yourself.

Coaching equips you with the skills that define strong leaders: a sharp instructional lens, a calm and credible presence, and the ability to influence adult learners. These are transferable skills, and yet, Black women are often passed over for promotions we're more than qualified for. But that doesn't mean we aren't ready—the system wasn't designed to see us.

To move forward, we must start by making ourselves visible. That might look like presenting at district or state conferences, co-leading school-based initiatives, or sharing how your coaching work has driven growth. Visibility isn't about self-promotion—it's about clarifying your value and ensuring it's seen.

As you step forward in leadership, mentorship and sponsorship become essential. A mentor helps refine your craft. A sponsor says your name in rooms you haven't entered yet. Start with your immediate circle—who affirms and pushes you to grow? Seek out those who understand your brilliance and context, and expand your circle intentionally. Community isn't just helpful— it's vital.

In many ways, you're already leading and shaping thought. Whether you guide teachers through change, push school culture toward equity, or advocate for student-centered practices, your voice matters. Thought leadership doesn't require a title. It requires truth, strategy, and a willingness to share. You can start by writing a reflection post on LinkedIn, cohosting a webinar, or developing a framework based on your unique coaching approach. Your experiences are valid. Your insights are needed.

If you're being overlooked for leadership, it's not the end. It's the beginning of your advocacy. Use your data. Tell your story. Speak your vision. Your work has already proven your capacity.

It's also OK to want more. To co-lead, to consult, to create. Start by taking on a school or district initiative. Step into meetings not just as support, but as a contributor with solutions. Build a leadership portfolio that reflects your impact—and then name what you want next.

As you rise, don't forget to reach. Whether recommending another BWIC for an opportunity, reviewing a résumé, or offering encouragement, your voice can open doors for others. That's leadership. That's legacy.

To help you advocate for your next leadership move, I am providing:

- **A Coaching Impact Tracker** to help document your contributions and make your impact visible.

- **A Data Storytelling Template** to strengthen your narrative and show how coaching drives change.

- **A Leadership Advocacy Script** to help you name your worth with clarity and confidence.

- **A Mentorship and Sponsorship Map** to grow your support system and move toward your next level.

Coaching is a powerful role, but it doesn't have to be your final one. Let it be your launchpad. Let it be your proof. Let it be your reminder that you've already been leading all along.

CHAPTER 5

Let's Talk About Feedback

In my coaching work across K–8 schools, I noticed a recurring theme: Teachers were often guarded when feedback came from someone outside their building. To address this, I created a 4-step feedback method that centers on care, clarity, and collaboration. This simple framework has helped me build trust and create actionable growth plans with teachers, and it's something I hope others can adapt in their own coaching practice.

What follows reflects the method I developed and refined as a consultant working with over twenty schools. It began as an adaptation of my work with teacher leaders and coaches at the district level and evolved into a process that felt both effective and human.

Why Feedback Matters

Feedback plays an important role in the work that we do as coaches. When looking for a definition of feedback, the dictionary defines it as:

"Information about reactions to a product, a person's performance of a task, etc., used as a basis for improvement."

When you provide feedback as an instructional coach, you are setting the stage for learning to take place and reinforcing your role as an important resource to those you support and lead. Proper feedback has to be honest and actionable to bring about positive changes in teacher practice and student learning. I know how important feedback is and why it matters—it can shift mindsets and affect the implementation of lessons that have been thoroughly discussed at the planning table.

This chapter aims to explore the characteristics of effective feedback, help you hold effective conversations to support teachers in developing and strengthening their practice, and guide you in learning to identify grade-level and school-wide trends based on your coaching walks. These trends should inform your next steps as an instructional coach and at the planning table. Finally, this chapter will help you navigate conversations with administrators with solution-based action steps grounded in what you've seen and gathered.

Holding Meaningful Feedback Conversations

We've talked a lot about how well you are received as a BWIC in your various roles, and that's exactly why I had to include a chapter on feedback. When I taught a coaching course at the graduate level, feedback was the most uncomfortable topic for students to engage in and practice. When I worked with schools across the country in my previous role, some administrators were even uncomfortable giving feedback.

In the twenty-plus schools where I used this method, the administrators and some district-level coaches often said, "They're eating up your every word," as I reflected on teachers' work. And it was true—but I knew I had just one chance to make a strong impression and a positive impact. I had to be intentional, especially since I'd be back to deliver more PD. I needed to know what I was doing. So let's talk about a few things you can do to prepare. And yes, being embedded in the same building or having the same coaching load makes a lot of this easier.

Just so you know, the first thing you want to do is be prepared for the conversation. Always take a moment to debrief what you've seen, clean up your notes, and reflect on the key areas you'd like to discuss. Make sure you are clear on what you want to say and ask, because if you aren't clear, the teacher won't be either.

Next, this conversation is an opportunity to continue building your rapport with the teacher or leader you're coaching. As you continue strengthening the relationship and trust between you, their guard will fall, hopefully leading to a deeper coaching relationship. You want the person you are coaching to feel like they can be open and honest with you in sessions, during planning, and beyond.

You also want to be strategic about the questions you plan to ask. Yes, write them out. Try to make them open-ended and ensure they promote a growth mindset. You want to come prepared with examples of strategies that might be helpful in the specific area you're working on. Even in a facilitative stance, you're still the coach, and they may ask for resources. Planning the conversation in advance ensures you can provide support and guidance.

If challenges arise, use the NURTURE model strategies we've already discussed to help you navigate or redirect. Anticipate potential challenges and plan around them.

Characteristics of Effective Feedback

Effective feedback includes key traits like clarity, specificity, timeliness, and constructiveness. It should be collaborative, not a monologue. Ineffective feedback is often too broad and lacks actionable steps for teachers to implement. As coaches, we want to ensure feedback leads to actual shifts in instruction.

To keep teachers receptive, we must genuinely be open, honest, and value their contributions to the conversation. Feedback isn't just a tool—it's a relationship builder. When done right, it deepens trust, strengthens practice, and empowers teachers to take ownership of their growth.

Step 1: Celebrate

Celebrations are exactly as they sound. We're thinking of one, two, or three actions or noticings in the classroom that you can celebrate. So, while you know what you're looking for when you conduct your coaching, are you looking for student engagement? Are you looking for teacher talk? How much is the teacher talking? How much are students talking? Is the teacher doing that heavy lifting? Are the students doing the heavy lifting? What's the level of questioning? You know exactly what you're looking for in the classroom.

So I want you to name a few things you can celebrate as you browse your notes. What are some things that you can celebrate from that teacher as you're in the room? I like to be very specific and grounded in numbers. So I might say:

- Seven out of ten students were engaging in the lesson.
- Eight students were engaged in the productive struggle.
- The teacher called three students up to share their work.

I'm trying to be factual in my statement more than opinion-based, but I'm finding things I can celebrate. If the students did the heavy lifting and were primarily talking, then I may be able to show that. If they had the appropriate tools, text, math tools, or whatever they needed to experience success, that's worth highlighting.

So that you can write pretty quickly.

Step 2: Clarifying

When I say questions, I've already celebrated teachers and told them I will celebrate some things I saw. I know I'm just in the room, and you're just in a room for a short time when you walk through class visits—whatever you call them at your school, you don't always get the full picture.

One way that I dig in with teachers is by asking clarifying questions. Sometimes my questions range from:

- "I know we had to leave out, and I want to know more. Can you tell me about what happened after we left?"

- "We came in the middle of the lesson. Tell me how you set this lesson up so your students could succeed in the portion we saw."

- "I couldn't see this—could you tell me more about it?"

All of those questions help the teacher see that before giving feedback, I want to ask questions about things I wasn't sure about or questions I had during my visit. The questions allow you to inquire about what you couldn't see in that short window.

Take a few moments now to reflect on your visit. Put in a few questions you might have for the teacher based on what you saw.

Step 3: Considerations

It is important to be mindful of your focus when you come into the room so that the considerations are targeted, but the teacher still owns their actions.

You aren't telling them what to do; you're maintaining that facilitative coaching stance.

First, you will want to note one or two areas of growth you saw in the classroom—a next step or potential next step for the teacher. After that, you want to give time for the teacher to reflect and share. They're already engaging with you when you ask questions. And now, as you give considerations, and I'll give you some examples, you'll want to allow the teacher to share their thoughts.

If they're quiet while you're doing this part, prepare a few questions that you might prompt them with to kick off the conversation.

Example:

- "I loved how you had students up and sharing. I wondered if there's an opportunity to keep the other learners engaged while that's happening, so it's not just a conversation between you and one student. Tell me, have you done that before? What are some things that might keep you from doing it?"

By sharing my thoughts, I've also embedded questions to help the teacher reflect.

Another one:

- "Your students were on task and engaged, and I love that. I think they're ready to come up and share their thinking with the class. I've seen a strategy work well where, while students are working, you walk the room and preselect the strategies you're looking for ahead of time. You can identify students who solved the problem using different approaches. If it's math, start with someone who used a concrete method, then move to someone more abstract. If it's literacy, highlight strong annotation and reasoning."

Usually, if I give something like that, I'll ask:

- "Do you have opportunities at the planning table to consider which strategies you will look for?"

If I'm their coach, we can build that into our next steps together.

So when you're offering considerations, remember to embed conversation and open space for reflection. That's how your feedback will be received with thought, not resistance. Take a moment to write down your considerations and sketch how you might approach that conversation.

Step 4: Commit to Next Steps

The last step in providing honest feedback is leveraging next steps. Based on your conversation, you will ask the teacher to share one action they want to implement. In my experience, they'll likely land on something we've already discussed because the conversation flows that way.

Sometimes, teachers reflect on something during the questions step that ends up being their next step. Or they may hear one of my thoughts and decide to move forward with that idea. Either way, we make a plan once they name the next step.

If their step is to be more intentional about selecting strategies so students can share their work, we'll discuss what that looks and sounds like. How can they do that? Maybe it's just having a sticky note ready with the three strategies they seek as students work.

Once they've thought through that plan, I give them space to implement it. I'll say:

- "I love this plan. I'm so excited to see it. I want to give you a few days or a week to try it out, and then I'd love to return to your room. When would be a good time for a follow-up visit?"

This gives the teacher a chance to practice. If it doesn't go well or they have questions, they know they can reach out before I return.

73

When I do visit, they're ready, they feel safe, and we can have a strong feedback loop.

This cycle, starting with celebrations, moving into clarifying questions, offering considerations, and committing to next steps, has been incredibly helpful in my work. I've used it with K–8 teachers and they have been receptive and engaged. You don't have to use it exactly like this, but the key is to make it a conversation. Include teachers in it. Don't tell them what to do. Share what you saw, offer reflections, and let them choose where they want to grow.

Now let's talk about using the data from these conversations to inform your work across grade levels and the school.

Using Data to Inform Feedback

One of the best things about holding coaching conversations or conducting coaching walks is the data you get from them. Jeff Weiner says, "Data really powers everything that we do."

As you reflect on individual conversations, I challenge you to consider this more broadly. First, consider the trends that are happening at the grade level. When I debriefed with school leaders, coaches, and administrators, I would plan ahead by identifying trends I noticed across the grade level. Whether you are doing this on your own or leading a conversation with a team, here are three questions I asked to reflect on grade-level trends:

- Are there any patterns in student engagement in each classroom?

- Are there any gaps or inconsistencies in implementing the curriculum or standards alignment in each classroom?

- What are the most common teaching practices being used in each class- room?

These questions, or similar ones, depending on the topics I was focused on, helped me to be intentional when reflecting on my notes for each teacher. From there, I could consider the strengths and growth areas for the grade level. This helped me talk to the coach and leaders about the next steps for grade-level support. That could be coaching conversations with the team, planning strategically for planning support, or determining the next area of targeted support. It also helped identify teams implementing the current focus well, who could serve as a model for others struggling.

Next, we would elevate the conversation to consider what this meant for the school. The coaching walk focus often feeds into bigger school improvement goals or areas of focus for growth. For those conversations, here is an example of three questions that I would use to lead with:

- Are there any patterns in the types of support teachers need across grade levels?

- What challenges or barriers to effective teaching and learning have you noticed across multiple grade levels?

- Are there any opportunities for collaboration and support among teachers across grade levels?

I loved leveraging this data to discuss overall professional development plans and next steps to intentionally support the school or specific grade levels with the same needs. This process opened the door to strategically finding ways to support teachers based on their needs rather than a one-size-fits-all approach on the next workdays. It left leadership teams with a way to support them as they plan for next steps. The principals would consider the following as they planned for school-wide needs:

- What are the common themes that emerge across all grade levels?

- How can we use the data to inform our decision-making at a school-wide level?

- Are there any areas of need that require a school-wide response?

Communicating Feedback to Administration

If you're a BWIC who doesn't have a leadership team to process trends with, but still wants to inform your administrator, here's what that can look like:

1. Review your data.

2. Create a document that highlights trends at each grade level and overall.

3. Use this data to propose action steps for planning support or internal/external PD opportunities.

4. Decide how to deliver this to the administration team— formal or informal. Either way, your intentionality will be appreciated.

You can deliver this confidently because it's about making ideas happen. This 4-step feedback approach—Celebrate, Clarify, Consider, and Commit—has been one of the most impactful tools in my coaching journey. It's not research-based, but it's deeply relationship-based. I've seen teachers enthusiastically return, share their wins, and invite me back to celebrate their growth. That kind of trust doesn't happen by chance. It's built through intentional conversations that affirm, inquire, and inspire.

As a BWIC, your feedback moves beyond offering next steps and shifts to changing mindsets, opening doors, and building relationships, all rooted in trust. You have experienced firsthand that coaching isn't about a script or checklist but about being present, prepared, and intentional. Moving forward, consider making feedback feel like a gift instead of a judgment. Whether celebrating growth or navigating change, your voice and questions matter. You bring care and compassion to each conversation. Reflecting on your feedback approach and your takeaways from this chapter, consider these questions:

- How will I make this conversation feel collaborative and not evaluative?

- How can I ensure feedback leads to action instead of overwhelm?

While you don't have all the answers, you do need to be clear and committed to your approach. When done well, your feedback doesn't just change a lesson; it changes lives.

III

Part Three:
The Journey Ahead

CHAPTER 6

Leading with Intention...Implications for Instructional Leadership

"I ensure I'm in the rooms where decisions happen, even if I wasn't invited. Sometimes, just being present changes how people engage with you." — Michelle

Michelle's words echo what other BWICs have felt: Leadership means showing up, even if that means opening the door for yourself. This chapter begins with some of the key findings from the study and a point of reflection for leaders. Then, we shift from learning about and understanding the experiences of BWICs to uncovering what these stories expose a need for or demand from those who build and shape coaching and leadership preparation programs.

BWICs Lead and Advocate Without Being Valued

BWICs are instructional leaders who advocate for their teachers and students while combating the deficit mindsets of their colleagues. They navigate the educational landscape while facing the duality of racism and sexism. As leaders, they often balance instructional excellence with emotional labor, advocacy met by resistance and shaped by institutional structures that serve as barriers. These conditions force BWICs to employ strategies to gain credibility in their roles.

BWICs encounter a wide range of experiences in their roles, filled with both positive and negative moments framed by their identities as Black women. These identities influence how they experience coaching and leadership in ways that differ from their counterparts. Participants spoke about advocating for systemic change through their roles and actions while consistently addressing tokenism and other challenges.

Jade illustrated the complexities of self-advocacy, especially when trying to maintain collaborative relationships within her leadership team:

"I realized I was giving grace to my supervisor, thinking, 'OK, well, this is a Black woman; surely she's not doing me wrong.' But just in reflection, I'm like, maybe I should have fought more for the things I let go. Sometimes, advocating for yourself is just as important as advocating for students and teachers."

Jade's words reflect a common tension: BWICs are expected to be bridge builders and advocates, but rarely are they fully seen as leaders in their own right.

Redefining Their Roles Is a Means of Survival

As participants redefine their leadership identity, they offer insight into the intersection of race and education, drawing from cultural memory and a wealth of personal and professional experience. While sharing their lived experiences, participants reject and resist the labels and stereotypes imposed on them by others, bolstering their expertise and redefining their roles despite opposition. The findings revealed that Black women continue to shape their identity in opposition to environments that marginalize them.

Each narrative highlights how Black women challenge the status quo and redefine their identities, underscoring the need to prioritize more equitable support for BWICs' diverse representation and career advancement. Confronting barriers directly allows

BWICs to challenge and transform inequitable practices and systems while continuing to shape their professional identities as effective instructional leaders.

Reframing Resistance

The challenges BWICs faced ultimately led them to resilience as they implemented coaching strategies and adapted their practices to overcome obstacles while still positively impacting teacher practice. The instructional coaches in this study continually adjusted their approaches to meet the demands of working in environments with predominantly white teachers.

Phalan shared,

"Building relationships helps me, and hopefully others, not confirm things I may already have in my mind. It gives me a clean palette, or at least I try to start with one."

Her strategy echoed Dannie, who explained,

"I try to focus on relationship building and being in spaces where you can learn more about one another and how we operate. That helps build trust."

Implementing coping strategies allowed BWICs to fight against deficit thinking in their respective settings.

Collectively, the need for resilience was a consistent thread in every interview. Participants emphasized that while their experiences differ from those of their peers, their ability to rebound is essential for their survival and to serve as visible sources of representation for the teachers and students of color in their communities. As the interviews continued, four participants shared that they remained in their roles, despite unjust treatment, to mentor others or to serve as inspiration for those who would come after them.

Networks Are Lifelines

Networks serve not just as support but as a strategy. For many BWICs, these communities are where they learn to endure, advocate, and survive. All BWICs talked about leaning into their networks or having a community of belonging to help them carefully navigate their challenges.

Ivy shared,

"Using my network of individuals with similar roles or who are admins, you know, I really lean on them when I do encounter a challenge. I lean on them to guide me in what to do, and oftentimes, it's—stay firm. Stick to what you know. Document everything."

There were instances where some BWICs expressed or reported feeling isolated without a peer in their school or district role. These moments underscore the importance of having a supportive network and affirm what participants shared about the value of community. Their experiences highlight the ongoing dilemma of existing in the role of an instructional coach while navigating racial and gender-based inequalities.

The contributions of BWICs must be heard and acted upon in meaningful ways to validate their unique experiences and to ensure they are considered in the development of policies and other decision-making processes.

At some point, every BWIC shared the feeling that they had to prove themselves to be taken seriously or to have their contributions acknowledged, whether by peers, the teachers they supported, or the administrators they worked alongside. Ultimately, the findings from this study underscore the urgent need to dismantle the systemic barriers and structures that hinder BWICs in their roles.

In the next section, I offer insight for decision-makers to purposefully shape coaching experiences, training sessions, and team structures, including those led by instructional leaders, principals, and current BWICs as they prepare to guide and support the next generation.

From Insights to Action

Meaningful change requires restructuring leadership training to address systemic racism while ensuring accountability. Although current attacks on DEI efforts present a significant challenge to implementing these insights, it is critical to advocate for systemic changes that ensure equitable opportunities for Black women in educational leadership by finding ways to frame leadership development even with political pushback.

Create leadership pipelines with built-in mentorship opportunities to empower and equip Black women for their next leadership role. AA reflects on the importance of representation in leadership and the need for more intentional recruitment in schools and districts:

Districts need to look at the makeup of their buildings and staff and see if it reflects the community. Having a Black counselor or coach would make sense if you have a predominantly Black school.

These efforts would develop the professional growth of BWICs and provide emotional support as they navigate various challenges in the role unique to being a Black woman in an instructional coaching role.

Offer meaningful decision-making opportunities at the school and district levels. Including BWICs in decision-making roles and processes prioritizes their voices and begins to move beyond tokenism and toward authentic influence and engagement. This means we are moving toward a practice that challenges the dominant white and male voices to consider the experiences of Black women when establishing programs and redefining systems.

Allow BWICs to lead professional learning experiences to validate their expertise and disrupt the biases and resistance, often questioning their credibility. BWICs' perspectives are shaped by their unique experiences and bring authentic learning while connecting with their peers. Creating the space and opportunities for them to lead learning experiences reaffirms their role and intellectual contributions in the field. This is essential. As shared throughout their stories, BWICs have repeatedly overcome being undervalued. Give them the platform they've already earned.

A Note to Decision Makers

School administrators and instructional coaching directors must create environments where their coaches of color feel seen, heard, and respected, not just present. Representation without a voice is a burden and emotional toll. Tokenism carries an unspoken weight but is still felt deeply. When teachers pit coaches against each other or question the role of BWICs, leaders must not stay silent. When BWICs are a meaningful part of leadership and instruction conversations, it is important and cements the weight and validity of their role.

When considering your feedback and accountability structures, check your biases. Reflect on how your identity, assumptions, and leadership experiences shape your views, engage with, and support coaches of color. Consider how their background and lived experience shape the way they coach and how you engage with them. As you reflect, ask yourself:

- Do I trust their expertise as readily as I trust others?
- Am I interpreting assertiveness as aggressiveness?

- Am I downplaying their mistreatment since I experienced the same as a Black leader?

- When they offer feedback, am I receptive, or do I overlook their contributions?

These questions aren't theoretical, but they do carry weight. They determine how BWICs experience your leadership and whether they are valued or quietly pushed out. This level of reflection isn't extra work. It *is* the work. Deciding to reflect is choosing to lead with intention.

CHAPTER 7

A Legacy of Leadership and Mentorship

As you may know, this work is deeply personal to me. If you've made it to this chapter, something resonated with you. Perhaps you are an aspiring coach trying to imagine yourself in this role. Or maybe you are an experienced coach who needs replenishment or refueling as the work has depleted you. You could even be a leader or ally, trying to learn more about the experiences BWICs encounter. Regardless of your reason, I hope you find something here that reminds you this chapter is for you.

A Note to Aspiring BWICs

If you're holding this book and thinking, "This is the work I want to do, but where do I begin?" I see you. And you belong here.

Becoming an instructional coach as a Black woman is necessary and deeply impactful. It's also layered. This work will require you to be confident, compassionate, skilled, self-aware, direct, and so much more. You will find yourself navigating systems that are not always built with you in mind, but by now, I hope you know that does not mean you don't have a place. You do. And you can lead in your way, with your voice, and on your terms.

You don't have to be perfect to begin this journey. What matters most is that you are grounded in your purpose and willing to be a continuous learner. Throughout your journey, there will be times when you question yourself or feel like others are questioning your presence. In those moments, I hope you remember that your lived experience is part of your leadership. How you've had to listen, adapt, speak up, or hold back has shaped you and how you will serve in this role.

You must find your people. Whether that is a mentor, a trusted colleague, or a supportive network of other Black women coaches and leaders, you deserve a space to be seen, heard, and supported. Coaching can be isolating, but you don't have to do it alone. Allow others to pour into you as you prepare to pour into others.

Above all, never forget that coaching *is* leadership. Don't let anyone minimize your impact or treat you like a fixer instead of a leader. You are shaping instruction, influencing culture, and guiding others toward growth. You are doing important work.

Coaching while Black is different. But so is the legacy you will leave behind. You already have what it takes to lead. You are more than ready. And we are.

Words from the Field

The journey of instructional coaching, especially as a Black woman, is layered and nuanced but also deeply inspiring. The participants in this study offered not only their experiences but also their hopes for the future. Their reflections remind us that this work is not just about what we do today but the legacy we build for those who come after us.

AA emphasized the importance of self-advocacy, resilience, and surrounding yourself with a strong network. That network becomes your mirror, support system, and a reminder of the bigger picture: student growth and equity. She reminded future coaches that professionalism matters, especially in predominantly white environments where one misstep can easily overshadow years of excellent work. Staying composed in tense moments is a survival skill and a leadership move.

Dannie shared her hope that she models strength for other Black educators. She believes in making decisions rooted in research and best practices, even when bias makes the work harder. Her message is to stay grounded and let the students be the compass because their growth makes the work worth it.

Sunflower believes in the power of a trusted support system. She encourages coaches to build a personal network of mentors and peers who understand the complexities of the role. That circle, for her, has been key to maintaining perspective. She also emphasized being selective about whom you trust. Documentation becomes protection and affirmation in spaces where bias and misperception are common. Her advice is practical—stay engaged in professional learning, be flexible in coaching, and know when to pick your battles.

Jade echoed these ideas and added that for Black women in coaching, there is little room for error. Her guidance is to be well prepared and grounded in content. Not because perfection is required, but because preparation is a powerful tool. She also spoke about the importance of boundaries. Being overly available can lead to being overused and undervalued. Jade offered one more reminder: Be careful with your vulnerability. Share your frustrations with people who have earned your trust, not just those nearby. Her outlet has helped her stay whole in the work.

Ivy's experience as the first Black instructional coach in her district taught her the value of visibility. Within a year, two more Black women were hired. She now understands that presence can disrupt assumptions and create opportunity. Ivy believes in staying current with best practices and being prepared. She sees documentation as a tool for accountability and a way to honor her growth. For her, visibility is not just a strategy but a legacy.

Phalan encouraged future coaches to lead from their lived wisdom. Though she once questioned her readiness, she grew to trust what she learned through experience and continued study. Her network, which includes women who affirm and challenge her, helped validate her leadership. She believes in doing good work and creating space for others to lead.

Michelle dreams of building support structures for BWICs across the country. She wants to create spaces for collaboration, shared learning, and collective healing. She envisions a community where BWICs come together to share what works and process what doesn't—and to remind one another that this work should not be carried alone.

These reflections are more than advice; they are mentoring passed from one generation to the next. They offer tools, truth, and trust for those just beginning. They remind us that coaching, for Black women, is not just a role. It is a form of resistance, legacy, and a movement.

Practitioners Guide

Leading Coaching Conversations That Shift Mindsets

*T*his guide is for BWICs navigating conversations that chal-lenge deficit thinking, shift teacher mindsets, and foster cul-turally sustaining practices. These tools center your voice, protect your peace, and influence instructional growth.

This may be one of the most powerful and challenging aspects of coaching. Many of us have had moments, I'm sure you can re-late to, when our expertise was questioned. Not because we lacked competence, but because of who we are.

That reality is difficult to navigate. Shifting mindsets while en-suring we're heard and protecting our well-being is a double bur-den. We often carry the weight of advocating for students and teachers of color while managing our own emotional labor. Coaching is not just about instruction. It's about influence, resili-ence, and navigating power dynamics. I want to open this guide by acknowledging that reality. I see you. I understand what you face. Now let's dig into how we can navigate these challenges with clar-ity, confidence, and care.

Facilitative vs Directive Coaching

As BWICs, we often toggle between guiding and directing, holding space, and holding lines. There is power in knowing which approach to use and when.

- **Facilitative Coaching** focuses on asking reflective questions that prompt teachers to think differently. It is useful when trying to shift beliefs or build teacher ownership.

- **Directive Coaching** provides clear, research-based guidance. It is often necessary when teachers are new, unsure, or resistant. This approach helps build credibility and provides clear next steps.

Example:

- **Directive:** "Try using this formative assessment strategy in next week's lesson. I'll help you plan it."

- **Facilitative:** "What patterns are you noticing in your students' engagement? What's working—and what's not?"

Redirecting Deficit Thinking: Coaching Scenarios & Prompts

Here are three common coaching scenarios you might encounter, with reflection-driven ways to redirect them:

Scenario 1: "These students just don't care."

This statement is often rooted in frustration, not truth. Use questions to guide reflection rather than confrontation.

Try:

- "Tell me more—what makes you say that?"

- "When have you seen this student engaged?"
- "What strengths does this student bring?"

Scenario 2: "Their parents just aren't involved."

Shift the focus from blame to inquiry. Help the teacher explore context and access.

Try:

- "What opportunities have we created for families to engage?"
- "What barriers might be impacting their involvement?"
- "Are our expectations aligned with families' lived realities?"

Scenario 3: "They just don't have the skills to succeed."

Center the conversation on possibility and support—not limitations.

Try:

- "What strengths do these students already show?"
- "What scaffolds might help them access the content?"
- "What strategies have worked before that we could build on?"

Culturally Sustaining Coaching While Protecting Your Peace

Culturally sustaining coaching means affirming student identities and honoring their communities, while also preserving your own mental and emotional energy. Here are three core strategies:

1. Validate and Affirm Student Cultures

- Encourage teachers to integrate students' experiences into lessons.
- Push beyond surface-level "diversity" and toward deep cultural connections.
- Help teachers avoid stereotypes and instead build authentic engagement.

2. Check for Bias in Expectations

- Ask whether participation, grading, or behavior expectations differ across student groups.
- Encourage equitable academic discourse and culturally aware instruction.
- Reflect on whether teachers' expectations align with student strengths.

3. Encourage Strength-Based Language

- Shift "they can't" to "how can we support them?"
- Reframe conversations to emphasize opportunity over deficit.
- Model asset-based thinking in every discussion.

Handling Resistance and Difficult Conversations

Resistance is part of the coaching journey. Your challenge is to respond without shrinking. Here are three key strategies:

- **Pause and Paraphrase:** Respond to tension by neutrally restating the concern. "It sounds like you're frustrated by student engagement. What patterns have you noticed?"

- **Document Everything:** Keep records of repeated pushback or microaggressions. Use documentation to protect your integrity and advocate when necessary.
- **Pick Your Battles:** Choose when to push and when to protect your peace. You do not need to engage with every challenge to prove your value.

Use this guide to:

- Lead equity-driven coaching conversations with clarity and care.
- Challenge deficit narratives using strength-based language.
- Protect your voice and well-being while making space for change.

Want to go deeper?

In the back of this book, you'll find:

- Conversation starters for strength-based coaching
- Coaching prompts to challenge deficit narratives
- Reflection tools to help you track your growth

Every coaching conversation is an opportunity to plant a seed. Some will grow immediately. Others will take time. Trust that your presence and persistence matter. You don't carry this work alone. You are shaping systems, and you are essential.

Additional Case Studies for BWICs

As instructional coaches, we often seek professional learning experiences to enhance our practice. We read books and attend webinars to deepen our understanding of content, pedagogy, and coaching tools. However, few spaces ask us to reflect on the layered identities we bring into our work as Black women. Even fewer opportunities allow us to pause, process, and wrestle with the nuance of our daily decisions. This chapter offers that space.

The case studies in this section are drawn from patterns that surfaced throughout my research. They reflect real and complex situations that instructional coaches often encounter, particularly those navigating coaching while Black. These scenarios are not meant to have one right answer. Instead, they are designed to help you reflect on the context, the dynamics, and the decisions you might make in similar situations.

Reflect on what feels familiar or unfamiliar as you move through each scenario. Consider what you would do, how you might respond, and how your approach reflects your coaching identity and leadership values. Use the guiding questions to explore your thoughts, strategies, and any tensions you feel as you read.

Let these case studies stretch your thinking. Let them help you deepen your awareness and sharpen your leadership lens. Most of all, let them affirm the wisdom you already carry.

Case Study 1: The Fixer Role

You are an instructional coach in a district that often turns to you to handle difficult teacher dynamics. Your leader praises your ability to "connect with everyone" and often asks you to "help fix" teams experiencing conflict. At first, you feel proud that your skills are seen as valuable. Over time, however, you notice a pattern: most of the teams you are asked to support have unresolved issues rooted in bias, power struggles, or inequitable treatment of students and staff.

You begin to wonder if your expertise is being respected—or if your role is being reduced to managing others' discomfort.

Reflection Questions:

- How would you navigate this situation with your leader?
- What boundaries, if any, would you set?
- How would you advocate for a more strategic use of your coaching role?

Case Study 2: Representation and Responsibility

You are the only Black woman on your building's leadership team. Teachers of color frequently stop by your office for informal coaching, encouragement, or simply to connect. While you care deeply about supporting them, your workload is already full. You begin to notice that your role as a safe space for others is emotionally fulfilling and exhausting.

In a recent meeting, your principal praised you for "building strong relationships with everyone," but you realized no one had asked whether the additional emotional labor was sustainable.

Reflection Questions:

- How do you continue to support your community without overextending yourself?
- What would advocating for better support look like in this situation?
- How might you talk about the emotional labor of your role with your team or leadership?

Case Study 3: Undermined in Meetings

During a data review meeting, you suggest revising an intervention plan. Your suggestion is overlooked, but later, a colleague repeats your idea, and it is met with enthusiasm. This is not the first time it has happened. You've also noticed that when you speak confidently, others describe you as "intense," yet when your white colleagues take the same stance, they are described as "knowledgeable."

You are beginning to feel silenced, frustrated, and unsure how to bring this up without it being dismissed.

Reflection Questions:

- What strategies might you use to navigate this moment?
- How can you balance advocating for yourself while maintaining professional relationships?
- What support would help you feel more confident and affirmed?

Case Study 4: Coaching Across Difference

You are coaching a team of teachers who are predominantly white. One teacher frequently challenges your expertise during team meetings, asking clarifying questions in a condescending tone. Other teachers seem to look to you for leadership, but this one teacher creates tension that makes it difficult to build momentum. You've considered speaking with her directly but worried about being labeled "aggressive" or "too direct." Your school leader notices the tension but has not addressed it.

Reflection Questions:

- How do you decide whether or not to address the issue directly?
- What role does race or gender play in how you are perceived as a coach in this space?
- How might you work with your school leader to create a more supportive coaching environment?

Case Study 5: Career Advancement Without Burnout

You have been offered a district-level coaching role that would increase your salary and give you a larger platform. The position, however, comes with increased travel, less support, and the expectation that you "hit the ground running." You are excited about the opportunity, but also concerned about the lack of infrastructure and the potential impact on your well-being.

You wonder whether this move will allow you to thrive or force you to stretch yourself even thinner.

Reflection Questions:

- How do you evaluate whether an opportunity is aligned with your values and needs?

- What factors should be nonnegotiable when considering new leadership roles?

- How might you advocate for what you need to succeed before accepting the position?

Epilogue

A Call to Action & The Future of BWICs

To the Black woman coach who's carried too much, fought too hard, and still leads with excellence: This book is for you. May it affirm your truth, challenge the systems around you, and remind you that although you are unseen by some, you are essential to many.

The Legacy of Your Work and What Comes Next

I hope you have enjoyed reflecting on our shared experiences as BWICs as much as I have. As we close this journey, we focus on the legacy of our work and what comes next. This final section is brief yet powerful. It ties together everything we've discussed and encourages you to consider your lasting impact.

Coaching, Leadership, and Systemic Change

Your work is bigger than one coaching cycle or even one school year. Each day, you leave an imprint on the teachers and students you serve. Some imprints will yield immediate impact, while others will take time. Every conversation you lead, every challenge you face, and every instance of resistance you navigate contributes to a systemic shift. Even if you don't see the change immediately, know it is coming.

As you lead, remember to protect your peace. This work is exhausting, and we all know the toll it takes. Navigating biases, microaggressions, disempowerment, and being silenced can wear on you. Sustaining yourself while leading systemic change is the key to thriving. Build a community of support, set firm boundaries, and recognize when it's time to leave toxic environments. Moving on is not failure; it's positioning yourself for growth in a space that serves you better.

As BWICs, we are not just leading for ourselves; we are forging new paths for the women who will follow. Whether you aspire to move into administration, district leadership, consulting, or an entirely different field, your work sets a precedent for future Black women leaders.

Consider the legacy you will leave:

- What systems will you disrupt?
- What spaces will you impact positively?
- How will you create opportunities for other BWICs?

I challenge you to do three things:

1. **Document Your Wins** – Keep track of your impact. Advocate for yourself with the same energy you advocate for others. No one can tell your story like you can.

2. **Mentor Another Black Woman Instructional Coach** – Whether she is a veteran, a newcomer, or someone aspiring to enter the role, mentorship is essential for sustaining progress. The leadership pipeline for Black women in instructional coaching, administration, and district leadership is limited. If we don't reach back, who will?

3. **Create Your Opportunities** – Don't wait for someone to choose you. Define your vision, develop a strategy, and step into leadership with confidence and grace.

Coaching Is a Position of Power

You didn't pick up this book just to become a better coach. You picked it up because you were ready to lead, disrupt, and build something bigger than yourself. Coaching is more than a role; it is a position of power, a stepping stone to influence, and a tool for systemic change. Let's be clear: This system was not designed for us to lead easily. As BWICs, we will encounter barriers, microaggressions, disempowerment, tokenism, systemic obstacles, and promotion challenges. But despite it all, we lead anyway.

Coaching was never your final destination. It was your training ground. Own your expertise. You are already a leader. Find your people, whether they are mentors, like-minded instructional coaches, or a strong support network. Make your impact visible, keep your receipts, track your wins, and position yourself for the leadership role you deserve.

Advocate for others, but don't burn yourself out. Push for change, but know when to step back. Protect your energy and redirect your efforts when necessary. Most importantly, we should reach back and create space for other BWICs to rise.

Real legacy isn't just about where you go; it's about who you bring. You are part of a long lineage of Black women who have fought, led, taught, and reshaped education, even when the system wasn't ready for us.

Now, you are next in line. Coaching was just the beginning. It's time to expand your leadership.

Let's go!

Appendix

This appendix provides additional tools, resources, and affirmations to support Black women instructional coaches (BWICs) in their leadership, advocacy, and professional growth. These materials are intended to serve as ongoing reference points that reinforce the principles of the NURTURE framework and help BWICs thrive in their coaching roles.

This appendix includes:

- **Coaching Tools & Assessments** – Frameworks for addressing bias, resistance, and school culture.

- **Leadership & Career Development** – Structured guides for mentorship, leadership planning, and personal branding.

- **Communication & Advocacy Resources** – Conversation starters, coaching prompts, and scripts to navigate difficult coaching situations.

Use this section as an ongoing reference. You can adapt the tools to fit your context, revisit them as needed, and apply them to strengthen your impact as a coach and leader. Scan the QR code to access the editable downloads.

School Culture & Bias Audit

Purpose: This audit is designed to help instructional coaches, particularly Black women instructional coaches (BWICs), assess the school climate, leadership dynamics, and coaching culture. It provides insight into existing biases, levels of instructional support, and the overall receptiveness of teachers and administrators to coaching. The results will help shape coaching strategies, advocacy efforts, and professional positioning.

School Culture Assessment

Goal: Identify the school climate, leadership dynamics, and inclusion practices.

Questions to Reflect On:

1. How would you describe the **general school culture**?
2. Does the leadership actively **promote equity and inclusion** for both students and staff?
3. Are **diverse voices represented** in decision-making spaces?
4. Do teachers feel **psychologically safe** sharing challenges or failures?
5. Are there **established protocols for addressing bias** and inequities among staff and students?

Scoring:

- **1 = Needs Improvement** (Little to no emphasis on equity, collaboration, or inclusivity)

- **3 = Developing** (Some efforts, but gaps exist in inclusivity and transparency)

- **5 = Strong** (Clearly defined, effective culture of inclusion and collaboration)

Leadership & Bias Awareness

Goal: Examine how leadership views and supports instructional coaching, particularly for Black women in coaching roles.

Questions to Reflect On:

1. How does leadership perceive your role as an instructional coach?

2. Have you experienced or witnessed microaggressions, tokenization, or biases from leadership or colleagues?

3. How are Black women in leadership or coaching roles treated compared to others?

4. Are there clear pathways for leadership growth for instructional coaches, especially BWICs?

5. Does leadership actively seek input from instructional coaches on school improvement efforts?

Scoring:

- **1 = Needs Improvement** (Lack of inclusion, significant bias, limited leadership support)

- **3 = Developing** (Some awareness and engagement, but not always intentional)

- **5 = Strong** (Supportive leadership that prioritizes equity, coach development, and inclusion)

Coaching Culture & Receptivity

Goal: Measure how well instructional coaching is integrated into the school culture.

Questions to Reflect On:

1. How do teachers perceive coaching in your school?
2. Do teachers view coaching as supportive or evaluative?
3. Are teachers open to collaboration and feedback?
4. Does the school provide structured time and space for coaching cycles?
5. Are instructional coaches positioned as leaders or are they undervalued?

Scoring:

- **1 = Needs Improvement** (Coaching is undervalued, met with resistance, or poorly structured)
- **3 = Developing** (Some engagement, but inconsistent implementation or buy-in)
- **5 = Strong** (Coaching is a respected, well-integrated, and collaborative process)

Analyzing & Using the Results

- **Scores between 5 and 10** → Major gaps exist in school culture, leadership, or coaching support. Advocacy and relationship building strategies should be prioritized.

- **Scores between 11 and 15** → Some structures exist, but there is room for improvement in leadership buy-in and coaching integration.

- **Scores 16+** → A strong foundation is in place, but ongoing adjustments may be needed to maintain momentum and ensure sustainability.

30-Day NURTURE Coaching Challenge

Purpose: A structured thirty-day coaching challenge aligned with the NURTURE framework, focusing on practical strategies to implement coaching effectively.

Monday	Tuesday	Wednesday	Thursday	Friday
Week One Goal: Recognize and honor the value of your unique experiences and expertise as an instructional coach.				
Define your *why* as a coach. What drives you to do this work?	Identify a time when your coaching made a significant impact. Write it down.	Reflect on your strengths as a coach. How do they shape your approach?	Ask a trusted colleague to share what they see as your strongest coaching skill.	Develop a short coaching mantra that reminds you of your impact and resilience.
Week Two Goal: Strengthen relationships with teachers, administrators, and fellow coaches to enhance coaching impact.				
Have a non-coaching conversation with a teacher to build rapport.	Ask a teacher what type of support they need most from coaching.	Write down three ways to make coaching feel less evaluative and more supportive.	Identify one administrator or leader with whom you need to develop a stronger relationship.	Send a personalized note or email to a teacher, acknowledging something great you saw them do.

Week Three Goal: Engage in self-reflection and continuous improvement to refine your coaching approach.				
Watch or listen to a coaching-related webinar or podcast.	Review a coaching cycle you recently completed. Identify a success and an area for growth.	Reflect on a difficult coaching moment. What did you learn from it?	Create or update a tool (checklist, observation form, etc.) to improve your coaching sessions.	Identify one strategy you will implement to improve your next coaching cycle.

Week Four Goal: Elevate your coaching beyond individual support by influencing school-wide instructional shifts.				
Identify a common teacher misconception about coaching and plan a strategy to address it.	Reflect on how you handle resistance to coaching. Identify a new approach to try.	Develop a personal goal for your long-term impact as a coach.	Identify your key takeaways from this challenge. What has changed in your coaching?	Write a personal commitment statement about how you will continue thriving in your coaching role.

Weekly Coaching Reflections

Wins of the Week: What coaching moments felt most impactful?
Challenges & Adjustments: What **resistance or bias** did you encounter?
Teacher Engagement: Who was **receptive** vs **hesitant**? Why?
NURTURE Integration: Which **NURTURE principle** did you focus on most this week?
Next Steps: What's **one small coaching action** for next week?

_____

_____

_____

_____

_____

_____

_____

_____

_____

_____

_____

_____

_____

_____

_____

_____

_____

Conversation Starters for Challenging Bias

Purpose: Provides nonconfrontational but firm questions to challenge deficit-based thinking.

Addressing Low Expectations

- What makes you say that?
- What strengths do you see, and how can we leverage those?
- How can we ensure expectations are representative of all students' potential?
- What supports could be put into place to help students meet high expectations?
- If we assume students want to succeed, what barriers might hinder them?
- What data supports the assumption that this student can't succeed?
- What instructional changes can we make to ensure equitable access to learning?

Addressing Assumptions Related to Behavior

- How might cultural differences influence how some students show up or behave in class?
- How can we involve students in creating solutions that might work for them?
- Have you noticed times when this student was engaged? What was different? (Shifts focus to strengths.)
- Have we examined our own biases in assessing student performance and engagement?

Coaching Prompts for Strength-Based Conversations

Purpose: Helps shift teachers from **problem-focused** to **growth-oriented** thinking.

Implementation Tips

- Use these prompts in coaching conversations, PLC meetings, or reflection sessions.
- Pair prompts with specific student data or observations to ground discussions in evidence.
- Encourage teachers to journal responses to track mindset shifts over time.
- Model strength-based conversations by using these prompts in your reflections.

Coaching Prompts

- What does this student need to feel successful in this moment?
- What progress have you seen, even if small?
- What's one small change we can make tomorrow?
- How can we reframe this challenge as an opportunity for growth?
- What shifts in classroom practices might help create more opportunities for success?
- What strengths does this student bring to the classroom?

- Assuming students are doing their best, what support could we provide?

Sentence Stems

- How can we build on what we've already seen by …
- What is one way we can support this student in feeling more confident about …
- I see potential here; how can we create opportunities to nurture that?
- Instead of focusing on what's not working, let's think about what has worked and …
- If we take a strength-based approach, what might we do differently here?

Framework for Coaching Difficult Teachers

Purpose: This framework provides a structured, step-by-step approach to engaging resistant teachers in coaching. By prioritizing reflection, active listening, and intentional conversations, instructional coaches can build trust, challenge mindsets, and promote professional growth while maintaining productive coaching relationships.

Framework Steps

Step 1: Pause and Paraphrase

Purpose: Establish understanding and de-escalate tension by acknowledging emotions without reinforcing negativity.

- It sounds like you're frustrated. Let's explore what's behind that.
- I hear that this situation has been challenging for you. Can you share more about what is making it difficult?
- It seems like some barriers are getting in the way. Let's unpack them together.

Step 2: Ask Reflective Questions

Purpose: Encourage self-reflection to move the conversation from complaints to constructive thinking.

- What patterns have you noticed when students engage with this lesson?
- How do you think your approach is influencing student outcomes?

114

- If a new teacher faced this challenge, what advice would you give them?

Step 3: Reframe the Narrative

Purpose: Shift the focus from problems to solutions by encouraging a growth-oriented mindset.

- What if we assumed this challenge had a solution? What could that look like?
- Let's imagine this situation six months from now. What would need to change for it to feel successful?
- Instead of focusing on what is not working, what small steps could we take to improve this?

Step 4: Set Boundaries

Purpose: Establish expectations for coaching interactions to ensure they remain productive and professional.

- I want our coaching space to feel productive. How can we make that happen?
- Let's focus on what we can control and shift our energy toward solutions. How can I support you in that?
- I am here to support, but for coaching to be effective, we both need to engage in solutions-focused thinking. What does that look like for you?

Implementation Tips

- Approach difficult conversations with curiosity, not defensiveness.
- Acknowledge resistance without reinforcing negativity.

- Use reflective questions to help teachers arrive at their solutions.

- Avoid power struggles by focusing on shared goals and student success.

- Keep the focus on progress, not perfection.

Resistance Response Framework

Purpose: This framework helps Black women instructional coaches (BWICs) assess whether teacher resistance is rooted in **discomfort with change, bias against the coach, or power struggles**. By identifying the source of resistance, coaches can tailor their responses effectively and maintain productive coaching relationships.

Discomfort with Change? Resistance often stems from fear of failure or uncertainty about new practices.

- **Response:** Encourage small, manageable steps that feel achievable.
    - What is one adjustment you feel comfortable trying first?
    - What support would make this transition easier for you?
    - Let's start with something small and build from there.

Bias Against You as a Coach? Some resistance may be rooted in biases related to race, gender, or perceived authority.

- **Response:** Document, redirect, and escalate if necessary.
    - What are your concerns about coaching, and how can we address them together?
    - Let's focus on the data and student outcomes. What does the evidence tell us?
    - What would success in this coaching relationship look like for you?

- o I want to ensure that coaching is centered on student success. What adjustments do you think would be most effective?

- o If there are concerns about my role, let's discuss how to collaborate to support instructional goals.

Alternative Approach

Scenario: A teacher consistently dismisses coaching feedback or refuses to engage in discussions.

- • **Response:** Redirect the conversation to shared goals and encourage reflection.

  - o I hear that you have some concerns. What is your biggest priority for your students right now?

  - o Let's explore what works well in your classroom and build from there.

  - o What would make coaching more beneficial for you if we adjusted our approach?

Power Resistance? Some educators may resist coaching due to a belief that it undermines their authority or autonomy.

- • **Response:** Reframe coaching as a tool for student success, not personal control.

  - o My role is to support, not evaluate. How can we work together to improve student learning?

  - o This is about ensuring students get what they need. How can we make that happen?

  - o I respect your expertise. Let's collaborate to find what works best for your students.

Data Storytelling Template

Purpose: This template helps instructional coaches translate their coaching impact into compelling leadership narratives by using data to tell a clear and persuasive story. By structuring data into a meaningful narrative, coaches can effectively communicate their influence on teacher growth and student success.

Section	Description
The Problem	Clearly state the instructional challenge, supported by data: What instructional challenge existed? What data or observations highlighted the need for coaching?
The Coaching Strategy	Describe the interventions and support provided: What specific coaching support was provided? What professional development, modeling, or feedback was implemented? How was teacher engagement and responsiveness measured?
The Results	Highlight measurable outcomes and impact: What measurable improvements were seen? What shifts in teacher practice or student outcomes were observed? What qualitative and quantitative data support these improvements?

Section	Example Descriptions
The Problem	Teachers were resistant to feedback and hesitant to engage in coaching cycles. In leadership meetings, instructional coaching was not consistently prioritized, which often required additional advocacy to secure buy-in.
The Coaching Strategy	I leveraged my relationships with key teacher leaders to gain buy-in and reframed coaching as a collaborative, teacher-driven process. I also incorporated culturally responsive strategies to ensure coaching aligned with the diverse student population.
The Results	After six weeks, formative assessments showed a 20% increase in reading comprehension, and teacher participation in coaching cycles increased from 30% to 75%. Additionally, leadership began including coaching updates in staff meetings, showing a shift in how the role was valued.

Section	Description
The Problem	
The Coaching Strategy	
The Results	

Section	Description
The Problem	
The Coaching Strategy	
The Results	

Advocacy Scripts for Black Women Instructional Coaches (BWICs)

Purpose: This document provides pre-written scripts to help Black women instructional coaches (BWICs) navigate common leadership challenges. These scripts are designed to empower BWICs to advocate for themselves, challenge bias, and secure leadership opportunities.

Implementation Tips

- Adapt scripts to fit your personal voice and coaching environment.
- Use data and evidence to support advocacy conversations.
- Seek mentorship and allyship within leadership teams to strengthen advocacy efforts.

Scenario	Advocacy Script	Follow-Up Questions
Promotion Advocacy: You want to position yourself for leadership opportunities.	I've successfully led instructional improvements and want to continue impacting teaching at a higher level. What leadership opportunities align with my expertise?	What steps can I take to transition into a leadership role in the district? How can I leverage my current work to demonstrate my readiness for

		promotion?
Addressing Bias in Leadership Perception: Your leadership contributions are overlooked or undervalued.	I've noticed that my contributions to instructional coaching are not always included in decision-making discussions. How can we ensure that coaching insights are valued in leadership conversations?	What processes are in place to ensure diverse leadership perspectives are considered? How can I better communicate the impact of my coaching work to leadership?
Advocating for Coaching Resources: You need more support, materials, or structured time to be effective.	To maximize the impact of coaching, I need additional resources and structured collaboration time with teachers. How can we work together to secure these supports?	What options exist to increase coaching visibility and support in our school? How can we adjust the schedule to ensure coaching is prioritized?

Navigating Resistance from Teachers: Teachers are reluctant to engage in coaching cycles.	I understand that instructional coaching can feel like an additional responsibility. My role is to support, not evaluate. How can we collaborate to ensure coaching meets your needs?	What instructional challenges would you like support with? How can I adjust my coaching approach to make it more effective for you?
Challenging Microaggressions in Leadership Spaces: You experience subtle dismissals or undermining comments in meetings.	When I share ideas, I've noticed they aren't always acknowledged until someone else repeats them. I want to ensure all contributions are recognized. How can we create a more inclusive dialogue in our meetings?	How do we ensure that all perspectives are equally valued in decision-making? What structures can we implement to track and credit leadership contributions?

5-Year Leadership Road Map Planner

Purpose: To map out your career trajectory beyond coaching. This is a working document to set clear goals, track progress, and refine leadership paths over time.

Leadership Goal	Key Questions to Consider	Action Steps	Target Timeline
Define Your Leadership Goals	What leadership roles do I aspire to? What skills or experiences do I need to develop for those roles?		
Develop a Visibility & Networking Strategy	How can I build visibility in my field and community? What conferences or panels can I participate in?		
Identify Skill Development & Mentorship Needs	What training or certifications do I need? What professional development should I pursue?		
Mentorship Opportunities	Who are potential mentors? How can I expand my network?		
Transition Plans	What do I need to do now to prepare for that role later? What steps do I need to take now to prepare for my future leadership goals?		

Five-Year Leadership Road Map

Purpose: To map out your career trajectory beyond coaching. This is a working document to set clear goals, track progress, and refine leadership paths over time.

Define Your Leadership Goals

What leadership roles do I aspire to?

_____

_____

_____

_____

_____

_____

What leadership opportunities align with my expertise?

_____

_____

_____

_____

_____

What legacy do I want to leave in education?

_____

_____

_____

_____

_____

_____

Build Visibility & Expand Networks

How can I build visibility in my field?

_____

_____

_____

_____

_____

_____

What organizations or conferences should I engage with?

_____

_____

_____

_____

_____

_____

Develop a Skill Growth Plan

What certifications, training, or leadership programs do I need?

_____

_____

_____

_____

_____

_____

Who are the key people who should recognize my work?

_____

_____

_____

_____

_____

_____

Personal Leadership Branding Exercise

Purpose: Guides BWICs in defining their leadership identity and positioning themselves for future opportunities.

- Write a one-paragraph leadership statement that captures your vision.

- Identify two to three ways you can showcase your leadership expertise publicly.

Prompt	Response
What's my coaching philosophy? *(Define the values, principles, and goals that drive your coaching work.)*	
How do I want to be known as a leader? *(Identify your leadership style, strengths, and impact areas.)*	
What leadership opportunities align with my expertise? *(Explore career paths that match your skills and aspirations.)*	
What legacy do I want to leave in education? *(Think beyond your current role—what long-term impact do you want to make?)*	
Who are the key people that should recognize my work? *(Consider stakeholders, mentors, and decision-makers who influence leadership pathways.)*	

Branding Statement:

Mentorship Mapping Strategy

Purpose: Identify the right mentors and sponsors to support your leadership journey. Use this as a structured plan to identify and cultivate key relationships.

Step 1: Identify Potential Mentors

- List at least **three** potential mentors (inside and outside education):
  -
  -
  -

- Why do you want them as mentors? What specific guidance do you hope to gain?
  -
  -
  -

Step 2: Determine What Support You Need

- Do I need career guidance, advocacy, skill-building, or all three?
- What specific challenges do I need mentorship for?
  -

- Am I looking for short-term coaching or long-term sponsorship?

Step 3: Develop an Outreach Plan

- How will I connect with these mentors? (e.g., LinkedIn, conferences, personal introductions)
  -

- What will I say when reaching out? (Draft an introduction message)
  -

- How will I maintain and nurture these relationships over time?
  -

The NURTURE Mindset:
Affirmations for BWICs

General Confidence & Identity	I am competent and skilled and bring valuable insights to my coaching practice.
	My unique perspective adds invaluable diversity to the coaching field.
	I am deserving of my position and every opportunity that comes my way.
	I belong in every space I enter and confidently claim my space.
	I am a continual work in progress; each step I take is one of growth and strength.
	My contributions help shape a more inclusive and effective coaching community.
	I am capable of handling challenges, and I learn from every experience.
	I embrace my identity and see it as a powerful asset in my professional journey.
	My voice is valuable and deserves to be heard; I speak with confidence and authority.
	I release the need for perfection and choose to celebrate my progress and efforts.
	I am not defined by my fears or moments of doubt. My resilience defines me.
	I empower myself and others by embracing and promoting diversity in all its forms.
	I acknowledge my achievements and accept compliments gracefully, knowing I earned them.
	Every day, I am becoming a more confident and

	impactful coach. I support and uplift other coaches of color, creating a strong network of mutual growth.
Counteracting Implicit Bias	I am committed to fairness and equity in my coaching practice. I recognize and appreciate the unique backgrounds and experiences of each client. I am open to learning about and from the diverse perspectives of others. I challenge my preconceptions and strive to overcome my biases. I actively listen and seek to understand before making judgments. I am aware of my biases and continuously work to mitigate their impact. Every interaction is an opportunity to learn and grow in my understanding of diversity. I embrace diversity as a means of enriching my professional practice. I am a role model for inclusive and unbiased behavior in my coaching. My commitment to diversity and inclusion strengthens my effectiveness as a coach.
Cultural Competence	I value the cultural backgrounds of all my clients and respect their diverse experiences. I am dedicated to building bridges of understanding across cultural divides. I am respectful and curious about differences and eager to learn from them. I adapt my coaching techniques to honor the

	cultural contexts of those I coach. I communicate with clarity and sensitivity, mindful of cultural nuances. I am patient and open-minded in all my interactions, recognizing the value of diverse perspectives. I am a lifelong learner of cultures and strive to expand my cultural awareness continuously. I foster an environment where all cultural expressions are valued and respected. I am confident in my skills to navigate cultural complexities effectively.
Overcoming Imposter Syndrome	I have earned my place here through my skills and dedication. My ideas are valuable and worth sharing. I am capable and knowledgeable in my field; I trust my expertise. Success is not a fluke; I am here because of my hard work and talent. I deserve my successes, and I accept them with gratitude. I am more than capable of overcoming challenges and reaching my goals. Every question I have is an opportunity to learn and grow. It's OK not to know everything; every expert was once a beginner. My growth is a continuous journey, and each step forward is progress. Mistakes are part of learning and do not define my abilities or worth.

	I am constantly learning and improving, which is the true sign of a competent professional. I reject the idea that I must be perfect to be good; I am good enough as I am. I celebrate my achievements and recognize my progress. I am resilient, and I trust my ability to navigate through difficulties. I am not an imposter but a deserving and impactful contributor to my field.

Sample Feedback Conversation (4-Step Framework)

Purpose: This sample shows how a coach might facilitate a feedback conversation using the Celebrate, Clarify, Consider, Commit model.

Step 1: Celebrate

Coach: Thanks again for letting me visit your class. I want to start by naming a few things I saw that stood out. Eight out of ten students were fully engaged with the task. You called on three students to explain their work and used their responses to extend the learning. You also circulated during independent work and asked some strong questions to push thinking, which is definitely worth celebrating.

Teacher: Thank you! I appreciate that I've been working on giving them more space to talk.

Step 2: Clarify

Coach: I didn't get to see a couple of things in full scope. Can you tell me how you set the task up before we came in? I noticed they were already working with manipulatives. Was that part of the intro?

Teacher: Yes, I modeled one example on the board using base-ten blocks before I sent them off to try.

Step 3: Consider

Coach: Got it. One thing I was considering during the lesson was the way students shared their strategies at the end. That was a great move. I wonder what it would look like to plan those student shares more intentionally? For example, if three students were chosen ahead of time: one who used a concrete strategy like manipulatives, one who used representational methods like drawings, and one who went straight to abstract equations. That way, students see multiple entry points, and it builds a pathway for all learners. Have you tried anything like that before?

Teacher: No, but I love that. I usually pick whoever volunteers first.

Coach: I totally get that, and sometimes that works well! This allows you to scaffold who goes when, so all learners get in. I can help you plan for it next time if you'd like.

Step 4: Commit

Coach: So what's one thing you want to try before my next visit?

Teacher: I want to preselect those three strategies and plan who I'll call up to share. I think it'll help my students connect the dots.

Coach: Perfect. Let's try that in your next math block. Want to send me your plan once you have the three strategies mapped out? I'll pop in again next Thursday to see how it goes. Does that sound good?

Sample Proposal Summary Based on Coaching Walk Trends (Grades 3–5)

Context: After multiple walkthroughs and coaching conversations in grades 3–5 math classrooms, the following patterns have emerged:

Identified Trends

- Students are using various strategies (concrete tools, drawings, abstract equations), but are not always being guided to see connections across strategies.

- Share-out time is happening, but students are often randomly selected, which can result in missed scaffolding opportunities.

- Many teachers are working hard to encourage discourse, but would benefit from support in the intentional sequencing of student strategies during the debrief or whole-group share.

Areas for Support

1. Planning for Purposeful Share-Outs

Support teachers in intentionally selecting two to three students to share strategies representing a concrete–representational–abstract (CRA) progression. This helps all learners access the content and builds conceptual understanding.

2. Teacher Moves That Center Student Thinking

Host a short PD session or planning lab on:

- How to listen for strategy variation during work time

- How to note students' strategies and select share-outs to highlight them
- Sentence stems or prompts to deepen student explanations

3. Model + Co-Planning Sessions

Offer a mini PD with:

- A short model of a strategy share-out using CRA
- A simple planning tool that teachers can use to identify student examples before instruction
- Time for grade-level teams to practice using the tool on an upcoming task

Additional PD Consideration

Explore bringing in an external facilitator or partnering with a math-focused organization to deliver professional learning on academic discourse. A targeted session could help teachers:

- Understand the impact of structured discourse on mathematical reasoning and student equity
- Learn practical routines and scaffolds to build more student talk into daily lessons
- Identify ways to plan and assess discourse intentionally, not as an add-on

This could be scheduled as part of a district PD day or included in a future PLC series with support from your leadership team.

PD/Support Recommendations

- Grade-level planning support sessions the week of October 23

- One short modeling opportunity per grade level before November 1

- Follow-up coaching conversations by mid-November

About the Author

Dr. Courtney Tate is an educator, coach, and author with over 17 years of experience in teaching, leadership, and instructional coaching. As the founder of AlignEd Coaching & Consulting, she partners with leaders and coaches to develop aligned, sustainable practices that support growth, build clarity, and lead to lasting transformation.

With a Ph.D. in Teaching and Learning, Courtney brings research, real-world experience, and a heart for transformation into every space she enters. Her writing and coaching are grounded in faith, purpose, and alignment, guiding women to rediscover themselves and the power they carry.

Courtney creates space for clarity, connection, and becoming through her devotionals, workshops, or women's events.

Stay Connected

Visit: alignedcoachingandconsulting.com or courtneystate.com

 **Email**: Courtney@courtneystate.com

Instagram: @ctatewrites

LinkedIn : @thealignedcoach

Facebook: @thealignedcoach

Interested in booking Courtney for your next event or coaching session? Scan the QR code to complete the interest form and take the next step toward working together.

Thank you for being part of the journey.
Stay aligned and keep becoming!

REFERENCES

Aaron, T. S. (2020). Black women: Perceptions and enactments of leadership. *Journal of School Leadership, 30*(2), 146–165. https://doi.org/10.1177/1052684619871020

Aaron, T. S. (2024). Black women's reflections: Navigating the leadership journey and making it their own. *Journal of Educational Administration and History, 56*(4), 465–481. https://doi.org/10.1080/00220620.2024.2311398

Agosto, V., & Roland, E. (2018). Intersectionality and educational leadership: A critical review. *Review of Research in Education, 42*(1), 255–285.

Aguilar, E. (2013). *The art of coaching: Effective strategies for school transformation.* Jossey-Bass.

Aguilar, E. (2020). *Coaching for equity: Conversations that change practice.* Jossey-Bass.

Alston, J. A. (2005). Tempered radicals and servant leaders: Black females persevering in the superintendency. *Educational Administration Quarterly, 41*(4), 675–688. https://doi.org/10.1177/0013161X04274275

Alston, J. A. (2012). Standing on the promises: A new generation of Black women scholars in educational leadership and beyond. *International Journal of Qualitative Studies in Education, 25*(1), 127–129. https://doi.org/10.1080/09518398.2011.647725

Blazar, D., McNamara, D., & Blue, G. (2024). Instructional coaching personnel and program scalability. *Education Finance and Policy, 19*(3), 492–523. https://doi.org/10.1162/edfp_a_00407

Bloom, G., Castagna, C., Moir, E., & Warren, B. (Eds.). (2005). *Blended coaching: Skills and strategies to support principal development.* Corwin Press.

Bocala, C., & Holman, R. R. (2021). Coaching for equity demands deeper dialogue. *Educational Leadership, 78*(6), 66–71.

Brown, F. (2005). African Americans and School Leadership: An Introduction. *Educational Administration Quarterly, 41*(4), 585–590. https://doi.org/10.1177/0013161X04274270

Browne-Ferrigno, T., & Muth, R. (2004). On being a cohort leader: Curriculum integration, program coherence, and shared responsibility. *Educational Leadership and Administration: Teaching and Program Development, 16*, 77–95. https://files.eric.ed.gov/fulltext/EJ794961.pdf

Carter, A. D., Sisco, S., & Fowler, R. M. (2023). Since we are, therefore I am: Ubuntu and the experiences of Black women leadership coaches. *Consulting Psychology Journal, 75*(1), 51. https://doi.org/10.1037/cpb0000227

Cespedes, K. L., Evans, C. R., & Monteiro, S. (2017). The Combahee River Collective forty years later: Social healing within a Black feminist classroom. *Souls, 19*(3), 377–389. https://doi.org/10.1080/10999949.2017.1390361

Collins, P. H. (1989). The social construction of Black feminist thought. *Signs, 14*(4), 745–773. https://www.jstor.org/stable/3174683

Collins, P. H. (1990). Black feminist thought in the matrix of domination. In P. H. Collins, *Black feminist thought: Knowledge, consciousness, and the politics of empowerment* (pp. 221–238). Unwin Hyman.

Collins, P. H. (1991). *Black feminist thought: Knowledge, consciousness, and the politics of empowerment*. HarperCollinsAcademic.

Collins, P. H. (1996). What is in a name? Womanism, Black feminism, and beyond. *The Black Scholar, 26*(1), 9–17. https://doi.org/10.1080/00064246.1996.11430765

Collins, P. H. (2000). *Black feminist thought: Knowledge, consciousness, and the politics of empowerment* (2nd ed.). Routledge.

Collins, P. H. (2001). Like one of the family: Race, ethnicity, and the paradox of US national identity. *Ethnic and Racial Studies, 24*(1), 3–28. https://doi.org/10.1080/014198701750052479

Collins, P. H. (2004). *Black sexual politics: African Americans, gender, and the new racism*. Routledge.

Collins, P. H. (2009). *Another kind of public education: Race, schools, the media, and democratic possibilities*. Beacon Press.

Collins, P. H. (2016). Black feminist thought as oppositional knowledge. *Departures in Critical Qualitative Research, 5*(3), 133–144. https://doi.org/10.1525/dcqr.2016.5.3.133

Combahee River Collective. (2019). A Black feminist statement. *Monthly Review, 70*(8), 29–36. https://doi.org/10.14452/MR-070-08-2019-01_3

Cook, D. A., & Dixson, A. D. (2013). Writing critical race theory and method: a composite counterstory on the experiences of Black teachers in New Orleans post-Katrina. *International Journal of Qualitative Studies in Education, 26*(10), 1238–1258. https://doi.org/10.1080/09518398.2012.731531

Crenshaw, K. (2000, November). *The intersection of race and gender discrimination.* Background paper for the United Nations Regional Expert Group Meeting, Zagreb, Croatia (pp. 21–24).

Creswell, J. W. (2018). *Qualitative inquiry and research design: Choosing among five approaches* (4th ed.). Sage.

Creswell, J. W., & Poth, C. N. (2025). *Qualitative inquiry and research design.* Sage.

Darling-Hammond, L., Hyler, M., Gardener, M., & Espinoza, D. (2017). *Effective teacher professional development.* Learning Policy Institute.

Day, C., Sammons, P., & Gorgen, K. (2020). *Successful school leadership.* Education Development Trust. Retrieved from https://files.eric.ed.gov/fulltext/ED614324.pdf

Desimone, L. M., & Pak, K. (2017). Instructional coaching as high-quality professional development. *Theory into Practice, 56*(1), 3–12. https://doi.org/10.1080/00405841.2016.1241947

Dillard, C. B. (2016). To address suffering that the majority can't see: Lessons from Black women's leadership in the workplace. *New Directions for Adult and Continuing Education, 2016*(152), 29–38. https://doi.org/10.1002/ace.20210

Evans-Winters, V. E. (2019). *Black feminism in qualitative inquiry: A mosaic for writing our daughter's body* (1st ed.). Routledge.

Evans-Winters, V. E., & Love, B. L. (2015). *Black feminism in education: Black women speak back, up, and out.* Peter Lang.

Fenwick, L. T., & Anthony, D. (2023). *Jim Crow's pink slip: The untold story of Black principal and teacher leadership.* Tantor Audio.

Forde, B. N. (2022). *Factors impacting instructional coaching implementation: Perspectives of K-5 instructional coaches* (Doctoral dissertation, Brenau University).

Foster, L. (2005). The practice of educational leadership in African American communities of learning: Context, scope, and meaning. *Educational Administration Quarterly, 41*(4), 689–

700. https://doi.org/10.1177/0013161X04274276

Fullan, M., & Knight, J. (2011). Coaches as system leaders. *Educational Leadership*, *69*(2), 50–53. Retrieved from https://michaelfullan.ca/wp-content/uploads/2019/12/el_201110_fullan.pdf

Fuller, K., Moorosi, P., Showunmi, V., & Shah, S. (2021). Editorial: Ways of seeing women's leadership in education—Stories, images, metaphors, methods and theories. *Frontiers in Education*, *6*, 781049. https://doi.org/10.3389/feduc.2021.781049

Gadamer, H.-G. (1989). *Truth and method* (J. Weinsheimer & D. G. Marshall, trans.). Continuum.

Galey, S. (2016). The evolving role of instructional coaches in US policy contexts. *The William & Mary Educational Review*, *4*(2), Art. 11. Retrieved from https://scholarworks.wm.edu/cgi/viewcontent.cgi?article=1044&context=wmer

Galey-Horn, S. (2020). Capacity-building for district reform: The role of instructional-coach teams. *Teachers College Record*, *122*(10), 1–40. https://doi.org/10.1177/016146812012201003

Gallucci, C., DeVoogt Van Lare, M., Yoon, I. H., & Boatright, B. (2010). Instructional coaching: Building theory about the role and organizational support for professional learning. *American Educational Research Journal*, *47*(4), 919–963. http://www.jstor.org/stable/40928359

Gibbons, L. K., Wilhelm, A. G., & Cobb, P. (2019). Coordinating leadership supports for teachers' instructional improvement. *Journal of School Leadership*, *29*(3), 248–268. https://doi.org/10.1177/1052684619836824

Giorgi, A. (2009). *The descriptive phenomenological method in psychology: A modified Husserlian approach*. Duquesne University Press.

Gooden, M. A. (2005). The role of an African American principal in an urban information technology high school. *Educational Administration Quarterly*, *41*(4), 630–650. https://doi.org/10.1177/0013161X04274273

Grant, C. M. (2012). Advancing our legacy: A Black feminist perspective on the significance of mentoring for African-American women in educational leadership. *International Journal of Qualitative Studies in Education*, *25*(1), 101–117. https://doi.org/10.1080/09518398.2011.647719

Grillo, L. M., Jones, S., Andrews, M., & Whitehead, L. (2022). A pouring into: Theorizing Black women's educational leadership through the Afrocentric epistemological lens. *Educational Foundations, 35*(1), 33–51. https://files.eric.ed.gov/fulltext/EJ1358861.pdf

Guy-Sheftall, B. (1995). *Words of fire: An anthology of African American feminist thought.* The New Press.

Horsford, S. D., & Tillman, L. C. (2012). Inventing herself: Examining the intersectional identities and educational leadership of Black women in the USA. *International Journal of Qualitative Studies in Education, 25*(1), 1–9. https://doi.org/10.1080/09518398.2011.647727

Hunter, S. B., & Redding, C. (2023). Examining the presence and equitable distribution of instructional coaching programs and coaches' teaching expertise across Tennessee schools. *Educational Policy, 37*(4), 1151–1178. https://doi.org/10.1177/08959048221087201

Johnson, N. N., & Fournillier, J. B. (2021). Increasing diversity in leadership: Perspectives of four Black women educational leaders in the context of the United States. *Journal of Educational Administration and History, 54*(2), 174–192. https://doi.org/10.1080/00220620.2021.1985976

Joyce, B., & Showers, B. (1982). The coaching of teaching. *Educational Leadership, 40*(1), 4–8. https://eric.ed.gov/?id=EJ269889

Joyce, B. R., & Showers, B. (2002). *Student achievement through staff development* (Vol. 3). Association for Supervision and Curriculum Development.

Karpinski, C. F. (2006). Bearing the burden of desegregation: Black principals and *Brown. Urban Education, 41*(3), 237–276. https://doi.org/10.1177/0042085905284961

Kendall, M. (2020). *Hood feminism: Notes from the women that a movement forgot.* Viking.

Killion, J. (2009). Coaches' roles, responsibilities, and reach. In J. Knight (Ed.), *Coaching: Approaches and perspectives* (pp. 7–28). Corwin Press.

Killion, J., & Harrison, C. (2006). *Taking the lead: New roles for teachers and school-based coaches.* National Staff Development Council.

Killion, J., & Roy, P. (2009). *Becoming a learning school.* National Staff Development Council.

Knight, J. (2004). Progress through partnership. *The Learning Professional, 25*(2), 32.

Knight, J. (2007). *Instructional coaching: A partnership approach to instruction.* Corwin Press.

147

Knight, J. (2008). *Mentoring, coaching, and collaboration.* Corwin Press.

Knight, J. (Ed.). (2009). *Coaching: Approaches and perspectives.* Corwin Press.

Knight, J. (2021). Moving from talk to action in professional learning. *Educational Leadership, 78,* 5–16. ASCD.

Knight, J. (2022). *The definitive guide to instructional coaching: Seven factors for success.* ASCD.

Kowal, J., & Steiner, L. (2007). Instructional coaching. *The Center for Comprehensive School Reform and Improvement, 1*(1).

Kraft, M. A., Blazar, D., & Hogan, D. (2018). The effect of teaching coaching on instruction and achievement: A meta-analysis of the causal evidence. *Review of Educational Research, 88*(4), 547–588. https://doi.org/10.3102/0034654318759268

Kretlow, A. G., & Bartholomew, C. C. (2010). Using coaching to improve the fidelity of evidence-based practices: A review of studies. *Teacher Education and Special Education, 33*(4), 279–299. https://doi.org/10.1177/0888406410371643

Mangin, M. M., & Dunsmore, K. (2015). How the framing of instructional coaching as a lever for systemic or individual reform influences the enactment of coaching. *Educational Administration Quarterly, 51*(2), 179–213. https://doi.org/10.1177/0013161X14522814

Muth, R., Browne-Ferrigno, T., Bellamy, T., Fulmer, C., & Silver, M. (2013). Using teacher instructional leadership as a predictor of principal leadership. *Journal of School Leadership, 23*(1), 122–151. https://doi.org/10.1177/105268461302300105

Nadal, K. L., King, R., Sissoko, D. R. G., Floyd, N., & Hines, D. (2021). The legacies of systemic and internalized oppression: Experiences of microaggressions, imposter phenomenon, and stereotype threat on historically marginalized groups. *New Ideas in Psychology, 63,* 100895. https://doi.org/10.1016/j.newideapsych.2021.100895

Neufeld, B., & Roper, D. (2003). *Off to a good start: Year 1 of collaborative coaching and learning in the effective practice schools.* Aspen Institute Program on Education, and Annenberg Institute for School Reform. https://files.eric.ed.gov/fulltext/ED480875.pdf

Neumerski, C. M. (2013). Rethinking instructional leadership, a review: What do we know about principal, teacher, and coach instructional leadership, and where should we go from here? *Educational Administration Quarterly, 49*(2), 310–347.

https://doi.org/10.1177/0013161X12456700

Reddy, L. A., Shernoff, E., & Lekwa, A. (2021). A randomized controlled trial of instructional coaching in high-poverty urban schools: Examining teacher practices and student outcomes. *Journal of School Psychology*, *86*, 151–168. https://doi.org/10.1016/j.jsp.2021.04.001

Robertson, D. A., Ford-Connors, E., Frahm, T., Bock, K., & Paratore, J. R. (2020). Unpacking productive coaching interactions: Identifying coaching approaches that support instructional uptake. *Professional Development in Education*, *46*(3), 405–423. https://doi.org/10.1080/19415257.2019.1634628

Shaked, H., Glanz, J., & Gross, Z. (2018). Gender differences in instructional leadership: How male and female principals perform their instructional leadership role. *School Leadership & Management*, *38*(4), 417–434. https://doi.org/10.1080/13632434.2018.1427569

Shirrell, M., Hopkins, M., & Spillane, J. P. (2019). Educational infrastructure, professional learning, and changes in teachers' instructional practices and beliefs. *Professional Development in Education*, *45*(4), 599–613. https://doi.org/10.1080/19415257.2018.1452784

Showers, B. (1984). *Peer coaching: A strategy for facilitating transfer of training*. A CEPM R&D Report.

Showers, B. (1985). Teachers coaching teachers. *Educational Leadership*, *42*(7), 43–48. https://files.ascd.org/staticfiles/ascd/pdf/journals/ed_lead/el_198504_showers.pdf

Showers, B., & Joyce, B. (1996). The evolution of peer coaching. *Educational Leadership*, *53*(6), 12–16.

Stanley, D. A. (2021). "I want to leave ASAP": Black women teachers discuss the role of administrative support and teacher turnover. *Journal of School Leadership*, *31*(3), 209–226. https://doi.org/10.1177/1052684620904021

Taylor, J. E. (2008). Instructional coaching: The state of the art. In S. R. Stoelinga & M. M. Mangin (Eds.), *Effective teacher leadership: Using research to inform and reform* (pp. 10–35). Alibris.

Taylor, K.-Y. (Ed.). (2017). *How we get free: Black feminism and the Combahee River Collective*.

Haymarket Books.

Tillman, L. C. (2004). African American principals and the legacy of *Brown*. *Review of Research in Education, 28*, 101–146. https://doi.org/10.3102/0091732x028001101

Tillman, L. C. (2005). Mentoring new teachers: Implications for leadership practice in an urban school. *Educational Administration Quarterly, 41*(4), 609–629.

van Manen, M. (1990). *Researching lived experiences*. State University of New York Press.

van Manen, M. (2014). *Phenomenology of practice: Meaning-giving methods in phenomenological research and writing*. Left Coast Press.

Woulfin, S. L. (2020). Crystallizing coaching: An examination of the institutionalization of instructional coaching in three educational systems. *Teachers College Record, 122*(10), 1–32. https://doi.org/10.1177/016146812012201006

www.ingramcontent.com/pod-product-compliance
Lightning Source LLC
Chambersburg PA
CBHW051315120626
46547CB00015B/2249